Canada in the Atlantic Economy

CANADA IN THE ATLANTIC ECONOMY

Published:

Forthcoming:

Trade Liberalization and the Canadian Furniture Industry

David E. Bond and Ronald J. Wonnacott

Published for the
Private Planning Association of Canada by University of Toronto Press

To William B. Lambert

These studies of "Canada in the Atlantic Economy" are dedicated with respect and gratitude to the late William B. Lambert, Chairman of the Board of the Private Planning Association of Canada from 1965 to 1967, who played a vital role in the development and supervision of the Atlantic Economic Studies Program, on which the publications are based.

His interest went far beyond his formal responsibility; he held a deep conviction concerning the importance of international cooperation among the North Atlantic nations. His untimely death came when the first draft studies had entered the early stages of publication.

© University of Toronto Press 1968 / Reprinted 2014 / ISBN 978-0-8020-3211-9 (paper)

Foreword

There have been two outstanding developments in international trade policy during the past twenty years—the multilateral dismantling of trade barriers under the General Agreement on Tariffs and Trade, which has been the agency for several rounds of successful tariff negotiations since its inception in 1947, and the establishment of the European Economic Community and the European Free Trade Association in the late 1950s. In a period of reconstruction and then sustained growth, these policies have helped the participating nations of the Atlantic area to experience the benefits of international specialization and expanding trade. The wealth generated by trade and domestic prosperity has also made possible external aid programs to assist economic growth in the developing countries.

Whatever the trade and economic development problems of the future, it is widely acknowledged that the industrially advanced countries of the North Atlantic region must play an important role. It is also generally conceded that the ability of these countries to maintain their own economic growth and prosperity and to contribute to that of the less advanced nations will be greatly enhanced if they can reduce or remove the remaining trade barriers among themselves. Cooperation among Atlantic countries is now fostered by the GATT and by the Organisation for Economic Co-operation and Development. But the success of these and other approaches depends on the assessment by each country of the importance of international trade liberalization and policy coordination for its domestic economy and other national interests. This is particularly true for countries such as Canada which are heavily dependent upon export markets.

The Atlantic Economic Studies Program of the Private Planning Association of Canada was initiated to study the implications for Canada of trade liberalization and closer economic integration among the nations bordering the North Atlantic. It is planned to issue at least twelve paperbound volumes, incorporating over twenty studies by leading Canadian and foreign economists. Despite the technical nature of much of the subject matter, the studies have been written in language designed to appeal to the non-professional reader.

The directors and staff of the Private Planning Association wish to acknowledge the financial support which made this project possible—a grant from the Ford Foundation and the contributions of members of the Association. They are also appreciative of the help that has been provided by very many individuals in the preparation and review of all the studies— in discussions and correspondence with authors, at the Association's November, 1966, conference on "Canada and the Atlantic Economy," and on other occasions.

H. E. ENGLISH
Director of Research
Atlantic Economic Studies Program

Contents

1. Introduction

Introduction*

Furniture-making is Canada's fifteenth-largest manufacturing industry. It employs more than thirty-three thousand people, with a payroll in excess of $121 million.

The furniture industry[1] is characterized by a high degree of dependence on domestic markets; less than 3 percent of total production is normally exported.[2] Despite the high existing tariff (25 percent), Canadian imports continue to rise in dollar volume and in percentage of total retail sales; the share of domestic market held by Canadian manufacturers is currently 94 percent, but it is declining by almost one percent per year. Both rising imports and limited exports suggest that with any reduction in the tariff the Canadian furniture industry would be highly vulnerable to import competition.

Five broad questions are addressed in this study: (1) Why are prices and costs now higher in Canada than in competing countries? (2) What are the prospects of the industry in a North American free trade area, and what would be the major impediments to its reorganization? (3) What are industry prospects under a broader North Atlantic free trade scheme? (4) What have been the costs to Canada of protecting this industry? (5) If

*Our major debt is to Paul Wonnacott, who in cooperation with one of the authors of this study first formulated the cost and price analysis of chapter 2. See Ronald J. Wonnacott and Paul Wonnacott, *Free Trade between the United States and Canada*, Cambridge, Mass., Harvard University Press, 1967.

During the course of this study, many people familiar with the industry were good enough to talk to us. Although our policy conclusions do not necessarily reflect their views (which were indeed quite varied), we are indebted to them for the insights they provided. We also wish to thank Donald Angevine for his assistance in collecting and evaluating much of the empirical evidence presented here.

[1]Furniture is defined as the movable articles in a dwelling, place of business, or public building. This definition therefore excludes some articles frequently considered to be furniture, e.g., kitchen cabinets, built-in bookcases. For a classification of furniture and the relative importance of each sector of the industry, see Appendix A.
[2]Data taken from Dominion Bureau of Statistics bulletins on the furniture industry, 1962, nos. 35–211, 35–212, and 35–213.

free trade is viewed as a long-term objective, which interim policy measures would be preferable in achieving this goal?

The changes induced in the furniture industry by freer trade will depend on a number of factors. The proximity of foreign sources of supply will determine the pressure on the industry to contract in the face of import competition, while the nearness of potential export markets for Canadian producers will operate as an incentive to Canadian producers to expand. The trade-off of these two conflicting influences cannot be determined without examining how free trade costs would compare in Canada and elsewhere. But one thing is clear: the importance of space in determining trading patterns. Furniture is a bulky item, frequently involving a low ratio of weight to value. Hence transport costs often prohibit its shipment over great distances. This is reflected in current Canadian imports, with more than 75 percent originating in the United States.[3] Hence Canada's ability to compete with the United States becomes a far more critical issue than the Canadian ability to compete with Europe.

There is another reason why the Canadian industry would be more sensitive to U.S. than to European competition: furniture is a taste item. Present Canadian tastes run towards U.S. styles and designs, as evidenced by the fact that Canadian manufacturers often copy designs from U.S. furniture shows; furthermore, the brand names that have wide acceptance in the United States (e.g., Simmons and Kroehler) are also familiar names to Canadian consumers. (Clearly the influences of distance and taste are not independent. Canadian tastes follow U.S. tastes because the Canadian public is subjected to the advertising of U.S. firms in the various media of communication. Furthermore, Canadian tastes are influenced by imported items on display, and most of these come from the United States, largely because it is the nearest source of supply.)

Taste factors would influence export potential as well as import competition. Canadian export sales to the United States might require some, but not excessive, styling changes, and the resulting product would sell easily in the domestic Canadian market as well. However, selling in Europe might demand a complete dichotomy between domestic and export production, with higher production costs as a direct consequence. Furthermore, Canadian development of sales organizations and distribution facilities would be easier in the United States than in Europe because of the common language and similarity in business methods.

It may be concluded that the prime issue for the Canadian industry is its ability to compete with U.S. producers; competition with Europe is of secondary importance and will be examined later.

[3]DBS, *Trade of Canada, Imports by Commodity*, 1964.

2. Present Canadian
and U.S. Prices and Costs

1. *How Do Canadian Furniture Prices Compare with Those in the United States?*

Price comparisons are particularly difficult in furniture. Two articles may have the same outward appearance but be built of components of entirely different quality. For example, one may be solid wood, while the other may be a veneer. Two sofas may have the same shape, but the upholstering may be different in grade and composition.[1]

In an effort to minimize this source of error, price comparisons were limited to products of two companies, manufacturing identical items on both sides of the border. Executives of these companies indicated that they used similar engineering specifications and wood finishes; to the best of their knowledge they knew of no quality differences in the items compared. (Because of the desirability of this sort of rigid quality control, this survey had to be limited to only two types of furniture, case goods and mattresses.)

The data are presented in Table I. On average, for this sample, Canadian prices exceed U.S. prices by 18 percent. It should be recognized that this estimate may be subject to substantial error because of the (admitted) limitations of this sample. Only seventeen Canadian-produced items are examined out of a total of more than a hundred thousand items produced by more than two thousand establishments. Furthermore, only Canadian subsidiaries are represented, rather than domestically owned Canadian companies, and pricing policies of these two groups may vary. However, fragmentary information suggests that a broader sample would exhibit price differences of at least the same magnitude. Indeed, there are several reasons for expecting that a broader sample would indicate an even greater excess in Canadian price. The two firms represented in this sample are two of the largest firms in Canada and hence may have lower costs of production than

[1]It is extremely difficult to control for quality differences in upholstery. One Canadian manufacturer indicated that a grade *A* fabric in Canada is at best a grade *B* fabric in the United States. In most cases there are differences in thread, the count per square inch, or the fibre used.

TABLE I

FACTORY PRICE COMPARISONS OF FURNITURE, UNITED STATES AND CANADA
NET OF TAXES, SEPTEMBER 1, 1965
(all prices converted into Canadian dollars)

	(1) U.S. price	(2) Canadian price	(3) Percentage Canadian price exceeds U.S. price
	($)	($)	
Case goods			
Headboard with heavy-duty metal frame	39.96	45.00	13.1
Headboard with heavy-duty metal frame	66.60	75.00	12.6
5-drawer chest on chest	121.47	145.00	19.4
9-drawer triple dresser	132.23	155.00	17.2
Night table	47.30	55.00	16.5
Headboard panel bed	27.95	36.00	28.8
Night table	25.75	26.00	1.0
5-drawer chest	66.11	72.00	8.9
9-drawer triple dresser	83.85	111.00	32.4
Panel bed	20.37	28.00	37.5
4-drawer chest	39.24	47.00	19.8
3-drawer chest	37.03	39.00	5.3
6-drawer double dresser	54.93	76.00	38.3
Bedding			
Mattress—tufted	50.26	54.00	7.4
Mattress—quilted	50.26	55.25	9.9
Mattress	36.28	37.00	2.0
Mattress	32.20	43.50	35.4
Average difference in price			18.0

many smaller Canadian companies. As international firms, their pricing
practices may be more sensitive to international influences. Finally, their
Canadian products are almost identical to U.S. items. Hence they receive
no "protection" from imports based on real or supposed differences in
quality.[2]

A wide variation in the excess Canadian price (in column 3) is one of
the most striking characteristics of Table I. Of the many possible explana-
tions for this variance, three have been emphasized by authorities in the
industry: (1) there may be large differences in the size of runs, reflecting

[2]A final reason that our 18 percent estimate may understate true price differences is
the more liberal payment terms offered in the United States. One manufacturer
offered thirty days net in Canada, but a discount of 2 percent if paid in ten days in
the United States i.e. prices of the U.S. items for fast-pay purchasers should be
reduced 2 percent below the figures quoted in Table I.

large economies of scale, (2) some of the pieces may be imported by the manufacturer, and (3) the amount of wood that is visible may vary, and much of this wood is imported into Canada. In any case, there is no indication that Canadian price is determined by applying a rigid formula to a U.S. price base. From the very limited evidence, it appears that the tariff may have a mildly progressive effect on the price: more often than not, the more expensive the product, the greater is the percentage excess in Canadian price. On *a priori* grounds this is not surprising: it seems less likely[3] that Canadian producers can capture (U.S.) economies of scale in expensive items with small markets.

It must be recognized that price is an inadequate indicator of the degree to which the consumer is less well-off in Canada than in the United States. In addition to a higher price, the Canadian consumer faces a narrower range of choice. For example, in September, 1965, Kroehler offered forty-seven different items in its "Del Morro" suite in the United States but only six items in Canada. In such circumstances, the Canadian consumer can enjoy the style selection of the U.S. consumer only if he is prepared to import selected items. This involves both a personal cost of shopping in the United States and an eventual landed Canadian price which exceeds the U.S. price by substantially more than the 18 percent indicated in Table I.

2. Why Are Canadian Prices Higher?

There are two necessary conditions for a higher Canadian price: (1) the industry must be insulated from foreign price competition by a Canadian tariff (or similar impediments to the free international flow of furniture); and (2) Canadian costs or profits must be higher. Both must be examined in any explanation of Canadian price.

A. THE CANADIAN TARIFF

The Customs Act of Canada, section 519, imposes a duty upon "furniture: house, office, cabinet, or store; of wood, iron or other material; and parts thereof not to include forgings, castings, and stampings of metal in the rough." The Commonwealth preference rate is 15 percent, the most-favoured-nation rate is 25 percent, and the general rate is 45 percent. For our Canadian-U.S. comparisons, the appropriate rate is the 25 percent MFN rate imposed on U.S. imports; this appears to be the maximum degree to which the tariff allows a higher Canadian price.

[3]This is by no means certain. One can easily postulate a counter example.

However, the existence of Canadian protection indirectly allows an even greater excess Canadian price. Notice from Table I that Canadian producers succeed in pricing certain items in Canada substantially above the U.S. price plus the 25 percent Canadian tariff. This implies that other restrictions on the free international flow of furniture are important. These include lack of information by the Canadian public on comparative prices and model availability in the United States. In addition, extra service costs are involved for a Canadian importing through a Canadian dealer; alternatively, shopping directly in the United States involves personal cost, inconvenience, and problems in avoiding the payment of sales or excise taxes in both countries.

Since the 18 percent higher Canadian price falls short of the 25 percent Canadian tariff, imported items are more expensive in the Canadian market than similar items produced in Canada. (This may be explained by price competition among domestic Canadian producers, or as a conscious attempt by these producers to divert Canadian consumption from imports to lines that are domestically produced, or as an attempt to discourage competition from other U.S. firms that might export into Canada.) But even though Canadian prices are not as high as the tariff might allow, they are still substantially above U.S. domestic prices. Consequently, Canadian unit costs and/or profits must be higher. It is appropriate at this point to examine comparative costs and profits in some detail.

B. LABOUR COSTS

These vary in the two countries because of wage and productivity differences.

Average labour productivity in Canada falls short of that in the United States.[4] There are indications that this does not occur because labour is inherently less productive, but rather because production for the smaller Canadian market involves inefficiencies in the allocation and execution of tasks. The difference in labour productivity therefore can be viewed as one component in a broader category of "inefficiency of limited scale," which is evaluated below.

This assumption of equal "inherent" productivity of the Canadian and U.S. labour forces is sufficiently critical to deserve further examination. In a survey of firms employing labour in similar tasks on both sides of the border, Young[5] found that Canadian labour was preferred in some respects ("more cooperative, less pampered") but inferior in others ("more

[4]This is generally true; exceptions are noted below.
[5]John H. Young, "Some Aspects of Canadian Economic Development;" an unpublished Ph.D. dissertation, Cambridge University, 1955.

leisurely, less responsive to incentives").[6] He concluded that lower observed productivity of Canadian labour was not due to a difference in inherent efficiency but was primarily because of the size of the market and resulting lower volume output.[7] A recent survey by Laurence Daignault of Dufresne, McLagan and Daignault showed that output per worker is now approximately equal in the most efficient plants in Quebec and the United States. (This suggests not only that inherent labour productivity is comparable in the two countries, but also that scale effects on labour efficiency have been overcome in some Quebec plants.) This and other supporting evidence[8] suggest that Canadian production workers would be equally productive in a free trade North American economy.[9] On the basis of this conclusion, only two differences in labour cost need be considered—the difference in labour productivity due to Canadian scale (discussion of which is deferred to Section G(b) below) and the difference in wage payments, to which we now turn.

Computing the impact of different wages on total costs involves two steps—comparing wage rates in Canada and the United States and deflating this by the importance of wages in total costs.[10] A problem arises in comparing wage rates because hourly wages vary greatly among regions within each country. Rather than take a national average, we used rates paid in principal regions of production, thus highlighting centres of strongest wage competition.

In Canada, two regions were selected—Quebec (centred in Montreal) and Ontario (centred in Toronto). Together these two provinces account

[6]*Ibid.*, pp. 77–3. Another possible advantage of the U.S. labour force is its greater degree of education. See *Towards Sustained and Balanced Growth, Second Annual Review*, Economic Council of Canada, Dec. 1965, p. 58. The most significant educational effects are likely to occur at the management and professional levels rather than at the production-worker level considered here. Thus the major complaint of Canadian management was the shortage of trained engineers familiar with modern production techniques. There is nothing in Canada comparable to the furniture-engineering course at the University of North Carolina.

[7]*Ibid.*, p. 86.

[8]Mordechai Kreinin, "The Leontief Scarce-Factor Paradox," *American Economic Review*, March 1965, p. 131; and National Industrial Conference Board, *Costs and Competition: American Experience Abroad*, p. 54.

[9]Even some of the "inherent" differences in productivity listed above may be indirectly related to the tariff. For example, labour may be less leisurely in U.S. plants simply because management, under the pressure of a more competitive market, expects more of its labour force.

[10]The specific formula used was: [(U.S. hourly wage — Canadian hourly wage) / U.S. hourly wage] × (Total Canadian wage bill / Value of furniture shipped by Canadian manufacturers). Value of shipments is used as a proxy for total costs. The only difference in the two figures is profits. For many analytical purposes, (normal) profits may be usefully viewed as part of costs; even if they are not, value shipped is still the best available indicator of total costs.

for about 85 percent of total furniture production in Canada.[11] The remainder of the industry is scattered over the other eight provinces. While British Columbia has a growing and important furniture industry (6 percent of Canadian production in 1962), it still lags far behind both Quebec and Ontario and was therefore not included in our study. The two provinces selected lie close to the largest U.S. markets and production centres. Consequently, they would be in a stronger position than the other provinces to export as tariffs fell: they would also be very sensitive to import competition. An examination of their competitive position will highlight the strengths and weaknesses of the Canadian industry under free trade.

Three areas were selected in the United States—the Middle Atlantic (centred in New York City), the East North Central (centred in Chicago), and the South Atlantic (centred in High Point, North Carolina).[12] More than 75 percent of total U.S. production is concentrated in these three regions.[13]

Wage comparisons between the two Canadian provinces and three U.S. regions are shown in Table II.[14] Ontario and the U.S. South have similar wages. Quebec wages are roughly 10 to 15 percent lower, while the two northern U.S. regions have wages roughly 30 to 40 percent higher.

The impact of these wage differences on total costs is shown in Table III. (Estimates for 1958 and 1960 did not differ appreciably and therefore were not included.) Except for the comparison of Ontario with the U.S. South, Canadian manufacturers (and especially those in Quebec) enjoy a substantial wage advantage over their American counterparts. If this were the only difference in costs, Canadian furniture could sell for *less*, not more, than American furniture.

Wage costs depend not only on nominal hourly rates but also on fringe benefits, e.g., vacations with pay. In Canada, the average worker gets 6.3 paid holidays per year, a benefit similar to that enjoyed by the labour force in the U.S. East North Central and Middle Atlantic regions. However, in the U.S. South, 70 percent of the employees get no paid holidays;[15]

---

[11]48.2 percent in Ontario and 36.2 percent in Quebec in 1962.

[12]The Middle Atlantic states are New York, New Jersey, and Pennsylvania. The East North Central states are Ohio, Indiana, Illinois, Michigan, and Wisconsin. The South Atlantic states are Maryland, Virginia, West Virginia, North Carolina, South Carolina, Georgia, and Florida.

[13]20.7 percent in the Middle Atlantic, 28.7 percent in the East North Central, and 24.9 percent in the South Atlantic. New England and California are the only other significant centres of U.S. production.

[14]For a more detailed breakdown of comparative wages, see Appendix B.

[15]Department of Labour, Ottawa, *Working Conditions in Canadian Industry*, 1962, p. 39; and "Earnings in Wood Household Furniture, July 1962," *Monthly Labor Review*, Department of Labor, Washington, July 1963, pp. 814–16.

TABLE II

AVERAGE HOURLY WAGES FOR PRODUCTION WORKERS IN THE
FURNITURE INDUSTRY, UNITED STATES AND CANADA
(in domestic dollars)

	Canada		United States		
	Ontario	Quebec	East North Central	Middle Atlantic	South
1958	1.39	1.22	2.05	1.98	1.44
1960	1.51	1.31	2.11	1.98	1.48
1962	1.58	1.38	2.16	2.13	1.58

Sources: Canada: DBS, *General Review of the Furniture and Fixture Industries,*
1960, *Miscellaneous Furniture Industries, 1962, Office Furniture Industry,* 1962,
Household Furniture Industry, 1962. The Dominion Bureau of Statistics defined
production workers to exclude workers paid on a piecework basis only. Production workers were 71 percent of the labour force of the firms responding to the
annual DBS survey.

United States: Department of Commerce, *Census of Manufacturing,* 1958,
and the *Annual Survey of Manufacturers,* 1960 and 1962. Hourly wage rates were
obtained by dividing total wages paid production workers by the total hours
worked by production workers.

TABLE III

ESTIMATED PERCENTAGE THAT TOTAL COSTS ARE LOWER IN CANADA
DUE TO LOWER CANADIAN WAGE RATES, 1962

	East North Central	Middle Atlantic	Southern Atlantic
Ontario	6.3	6.1	0.0
Quebec	8.5	8.3	3.0

accordingly, southern wage figures should be lowered by 2½ to 3 cents per
hour prior to comparison with other regions. In Canada and the U.S.
North, virtually all employers provide at least one week of paid vacation.
But in the southern states 12 percent of the employees do not enjoy this
benefit. In comparative terms, this lowers southern wages by an insignificant
amount, i.e., about ⅓ cent per hour. Both these considerations improve the
relative position of the U.S. South, reducing its disadvantage vis-à-vis
Quebec and placing it in a slightly preferred position vis-à-vis Ontario.

These and subsequent cost calculations are based on the assumption of a
parity rate of exchange ($1 U.S. = $1 Canadian). It is difficult to project
exchange rates into the future, especially in the face of the substantial
changes in commercial policy considered in this study. Our estimates are

therefore on the conservative side; they apply even if the Canadian dollar rises to parity. If it remains at its present level, then the Canadian industry would enjoy the additional competitive advantage of paying wages in less expensive dollars. This would be equivalent (in 1962) to 10 to 12 cents per hour, or 2–2½ percent of total costs.

Wage differences and their resulting effect on total costs are brought into perspective in Table IV.

TABLE IV

WAGE DIFFERENCES AND THEIR IMPACT ON TOTAL COSTS, 1962

Wage differences (from Table II)		Cost differences (from Table III)
30 to 40% above Ontario ———	U.S. Middle Atlantic and East North Central	——— 6% above Ontario
0 ———	Ontario U.S. South	——— 0
15% below Ontario ———	Quebec	——— 3% below Ontario

Sources: Tables II and III

C. TRANSPORT COSTS ON INPUTS

Input costs of U.S. and Canadian producers may vary for three reasons. First, inputs may be subject to different government taxes or tariffs in the two countries; these influences are considered in section F below. Second, inputs may vary in price at different sources; information on this is exceedingly difficult to acquire. Finally, input costs may vary because some furniture producers are closer to input sources than others; transport cost differences of this kind are examined in this section.

Major furniture inputs were identified, along with the major sources of supply.[16] Not surprisingly, it turned out that Canadian producers were

[16]Inputs for the industry are listed in the DBS sources cited for Table I above.

closer to important input supplies than U.S. producers. Rail rates were applied to these data to determine the total cost advantage of Toronto and Montreal over the three U.S. locations.[17] The results are displayed in Table V.

TABLE V

ESTIMATED PERCENTAGE THAT TOTAL COSTS ARE LOWER IN CANADIAN
LOCATIONS BECAUSE OF PROXIMITY TO INPUT SUPPLIES (T_m)

	Chicago	New York	High Point
Toronto	2.01	1.92	.41
Montreal	1.74	1.65	.15

Proximity to input supplies (like favourable wage rates) is a reason why Canadian prices might be *lower* than those in the United States. Since our original objective was to explain Canadian price that is observed to be *higher*, we seem to be making progress in the wrong direction. A consideration of our strategy is therefore in order.

D. A DIGRESSION: A GRAPHIC PRESENTATION OF COMPARATIVE COSTS

Our price and cost estimates are assembled in Figure 1. For purposes of illustration only, the Toronto-Chicago comparison is shown in this diagram. (Similar comparisons of Toronto with the other two U.S. regions, and Montreal with all three U.S. regions, are presented later.)

The heavy horizontal reference line in this figure is the factory price of U.S. furniture. Higher or lower Canadian prices and costs are measured, respectively, above or below this U.S. base line. Reading from left to right, the first bar (D) represents the Canadian tariff of 25 percent—an index of the direct price protection provided to the furniture industry. Percentage P is our best estimate of the amount of this protection the industry in fact

---

[17]The formula for estimating T_m in the jth column and kth row of Table V was:
$$\Sigma^n_{i=1} (Z_{ij} - Z_{ik}) R_i A_i$$
in which:
Z_{ij} refers to the distance in miles of U.S. centre of furniture manufacturing j ($j =$ High Point, Chicago, or New York) from its most likely source of input i.
Z_{ik} refers to the distance in miles of Canadian centre of furniture manufacturing k ($k =$ Toronto or Montreal) from its most likely source of supply of input i.
Sources of supply were obtained from U.S. *Census of Manufacturing 1958*, U.S. *Annual Survey of Manufacturing*, 1960, 1961, and 1962, and DBS industry surveys.
R_i refers to the cost of shipping $1 worth of input i for one mile as determined from waybill statistics.
A_i refers to the proportion of costs of furniture manufacture devoted to the purchase of input i.

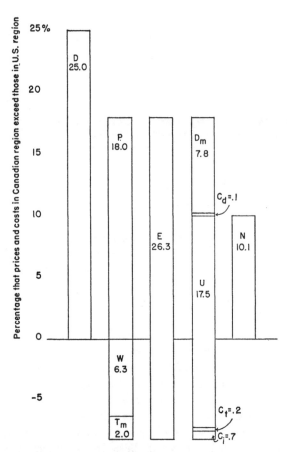

Figure 1. Comparison of Prices and Costs, 1962:
Ontario (Toronto) *vs*. East North Central (Chicago)

uses—i.e., the 18 percent higher price charged, on average, in the Canadian market.

There are two other advantages (in addition to their higher price) that Canadian producers enjoy. Their total costs are lower by 6.3 percent because of lower wages (W), and lower by 2 percent because of proximity to input supplies (T_m). Since both represent lower Canadian costs, they are entered in this diagram below the U.S. reference line. Terms P, W, and T_m all represent advantages enjoyed by Canadian producers selling in the Canadian market. Their sum ($E = 26.3$ percent) represents the margin that must be explained—in terms of other costs that are higher in Canada and/or higher Canadian profits. Canadian costs are shown in the next column in Figure 1; to their evaluation we now turn.

E. HIGHER CANADIAN CAPITAL COSTS

Higher interest rates in Canada increase the cost of borrowing; the impact on total manufacturing costs (C_i) was estimated in several steps.[18]

First, the total amount of bank loans, mortgage debt, and capital stock outstanding was calculated.[19] Each of these elements was multiplied by the differential between the relevant Canadian and U.S. rates.[20] These figures were then summed and divided by the total value of furniture shipped. The results of these calculations are displayed in Table VI.[21] Only a single Canadian-U.S. comparison is shown. A regional breakdown of this cost (like many of the others that follow) is unnecessary, since firms in various regions in either country have access to the same capital market.

TABLE VI

ESTIMATED PERCENTAGE THAT CANADIAN TOTAL COSTS WERE HIGHER
THAN IN THE UNITED STATES BECAUSE OF HIGHER CAPITAL COSTS

	1958	1960	1962
Effect of higher interest rate and return on equity (C_t)	0.84	0.81	0.68

Another higher Canadian capital cost has received a great deal of attention recently—the 11 percent sales tax on buildings and machinery (C_t). The effect of this tax was computed by applying the 11 percent tax to the industry's total expenditure on machinery and part of its spending on new plant[22] in 1962.[23] The estimated differential was only about 0.2 percent

[18]The rationale of our estimating procedure has been discussed at length in Wonnacott and Wonnacott, *Free Trade*, chap. VIII, and is consequently not reproduced here.
[19]From information taken from tax data published by the Department of Revenue.
[20]The appropriate rate for bank loans was the difference between the Canadian and U.S. prime rates. For bond debt, we used the average rate of return on ten Canadian industrial bonds (compiled by McLeod, Young, Weir) less the equivalent U.S. rate of return on Moody's AAA bonds. This differential was doubled before being applied to equity. (It was assumed that *after-tax* returns to equity in Canada would exceed U.S. levels by the Canadian-U.S. interest differential. With a corporate profit tax of 50 percent, the excess in *before-tax* returns would have to be double this.)
[21]These estimates are very tentative. While the prime rate is applicable to the loans of the large firms in the United States, the small, family-owned firms in the Canadian industry may not be able to obtain funds at the prime rate. Hence the cost of bank-loan capital in Canada may be understated. On the other hand, the required rate of return on equity capital in Canada may be overstated. Frequently family fortunes are locked into Canadian firms. The inability or unwillingness of the owners to exit from the industry may induce them to accept a lower rate of return than the average industrial enterprise.
[22]Only part of building costs (i.e., building materials) is subject to this tax; labour and many other costs of construction are not.
[23]Cf. n. 30, for reasons why this procedure is not the ideal procedure for estimating cost differences on capital inputs. Any bias in our method, however, is more likely than not to overstate cost effects, which are insignificant in any case.

of total costs; it is evident that the limited capital requirements of this industry prevent this tax from being a major influence on costs. Moreover, with the abolition of a portion of this tax on machinery in the 1966 budget, over one-fourth of this cost will disappear, and the removal of the remaining tax on building materials is certain.[24]

F. HIGHER CANADIAN FURNITURE COSTS DUE TO PROTECTION ON INPUTS
There are two reasons why furniture costs may be raised because of Canadian tariff protection on material inputs (e.g., foam rubber). First, foam rubber that is actually imported will be more costly by the amount of the tariff. Second, the price of domestically produced rubber may be higher because of the protection it receives; this will occur if the Canadian rubber industry takes advantage of this tariff when pricing its product.

Two different measures were used to determine how much the cost of furniture is raised by protection. One, a minimum estimate, assumed that Canadian input prices were higher only on goods that were in fact imported. Each furniture input listed in the DBS publications was taken separately. The ratio of imports of this good to total Canadian consumption was determined, and this figure was assumed also to apply to purchases by the furniture industry. Thus, if one-ninth of total foam rubber used in Canada was imported, it was assumed that one-ninth of the foam rubber used by the furniture industry was imported. Appropriate tariff rates were applied to all such computed imports[25] of the furniture industry, yielding an estimate of the total increased cost of inputs resulting from all tariffs. This figure, expressed as a percentage of total furniture costs, is shown in the first row of Table VII.

Interviews with manufacturers led us to believe that these minimum estimates were far too low.[26] For the maximum estimate, it was assumed that prices of all inputs—whether imported or domestically produced— fully reflected the protection they received. Many firms in the industry indicated that this was the case, particularly for textiles, plastic laminates, and plastic covers for dinette suites. The higher (protected) price was applied to all inputs regardless of their source; this yielded an estimate of the total increase in costs resulting from protection. This figure, expressed as a percentage of total furniture costs, is shown in the second row of

[24]See budget speech of Honourable Mitchell Sharp, March 29, 1966, House of Commons Debates, p. 3386.
[25]There was a problem in assigning the correct tariff to each input. For example, import data refer to "plastic sheeting," yet the Customs Act refers not to plastic sheeting in general but to a wide variety of specific types of sheeting varying in width, composition, and use.
[26]On theoretical grounds, the assumptions involved are inconsistent with competitive markets: similar products are assumed to sell in the Canadian market at differing prices (i.e., imports are higher priced than domestic products).

TABLE VII

ESTIMATED PERCENTAGE THAT TOTAL COSTS ARE HIGHER IN CANADA
DUE TO PROTECTION ON INPUTS

	1958	1960	1962
Effect of protection on material			
inputs (D_m): minimum	0.48	0.52	0.66
maximum	6.72	6.68	7.79
Effect of protection on			
machinery (C_d)	0.10	0.12	0.11

Table VII. Since our interviews with manufacturers indicated that this maximum estimate was closer to the mark than the minimum estimate, it is used throughout for comparative purposes.[27] It is used for another reason. Canadian protection not only has a price effect; it also restricts variety. Our maximum estimate of the price effect is used as a proxy for both disadvantages facing Canadian manufacturers.

In passing, it is interesting to note that the Canadian case-goods industry imports a high percentage of the hardwoods it uses on exterior surfaces. This includes not only exotic woods like teak and pecan, but also woods native to Canada, such as birch and maple. There are two reasons. First, in many parts of Canada woods are marred by a mineral streaking that is almost impossible to remove. Second, forestry management in Canada often favours the pulp and paper industry at the expense of hardwood lumbering. Pulp and paper companies with exclusive cutting rights to northern forests generally cut all wood within their region, regardless of size.[28]

Machinery is another input of the industry which is more expensive in Canada because of protection. Only a maximum estimate (in the last row of Table VII) was computed for this item; because this is so small, it was unnecessary to consider a minimum. An average tariff rate for machinery imports[29] was applied to the total expenditure by the furniture industry on (domestic and imported) machinery.[30] Since even our low estimate has an

[27]The choice of this maximum estimate is not critical in analyzing the impact of a general movement towards free trade. It becomes important only if single-industry schemes are considered.

[28]Recent events in Quebec suggest a change in this policy.

[29]Derived from *Trade of Canada: Imports*, 1958. A tariff rate was computed by comparing the imports by the furniture industry with the tariff revenue collected on these same imports. (The latter figure was available only for 1958; hence, the 1958 tariff rate computed in this way was also used in the 1960 and 1962 calculations.)

[30]Since machinery is a capital, rather than a material, input, it should ideally be treated differently—i.e., the higher price (in the year in which each machine was purchased) should be applied to its depreciation in the year studied. Our method, however, is a good approximation—although in a period of growth it will tend to overstate true costs.

upward bias, it must be concluded that this cost is normally a relatively insignificant influence in this industry.

Both these higher input costs (D_m and C_d) help to explain how the total Canadian advantage (E) is dissipated. Moreover, like the higher protected Canadian price (P), these elements of higher Canadian cost would disappear in any general move to across-the-board free trade. Hence these items are entered in Figure 1, opposite P. The net protection that the furniture industry uses is now evident and is graphically represented by N: this is simply the higher output price charged because of the furniture tariff (P) less the higher cost the industry faces because of protection on its inputs (D_m and C_d). Even though nominal protection for the industry is a 25 percent tariff, the net protection producers actually use is only 10 percent.

G. INEFFICIENCIES OF MARKET SIZE

When E (the sum of all Canadian advantages) has been reduced by all the Canadian disadvantages identified above, a large residual (U) remains. This can be explained only by higher Canadian profit or by some higher Canadian cost as yet unidentified.

(a) *Are Canadian profits higher?* Specifically, do manufacturers exercise more market power in Canada and quote a high price in order to raise profit levels above those in the United States?

The large number of small establishments in the industry does not suggest a concentration of market power. Nor is this indicated by concentration ratios of the industry.[31] While there are some two thousand establishments in Canada producing furniture, eighty-three of them do more than 42 percent of the total business. Each of these eighty-three establishments had sales in 1962 between $1 million and $5 million. Any effective collusion by such a large number of firms of roughly equal size would be unlikely to escape the notice of the Restrictive Trade Practices Commission.

The exercise of market power in Canada can also be tested by examining profit rates. While there are some very profitable firms in the industry, average profits are low. The return on equity (total common and preferred stock and retained earnings) in 1961 was 4.5 percent. The comparable return on equity for all manufacturing enterprise in Canada was 6.2 percent.[32] Since the industry return is below average for Canada, it may be concluded that excessive profits do not accrue to furniture-makers. Nor does their profit exceed that in the United States. In 1960, after-tax profit,

[31]I.e., the percentage of business held by the largest firms.
[32]Department of Industry and the *Canadian Handbook*.

expressed as a return on equity, was 6.4 percent in U.S. furniture-making,[33] compared with 4.5 percent in Canada.

(b) *Effects of a restricted market on costs.* Since there is no evidence of higher profit in Canada, our residual U is attributed to the one remaining explanation: inefficiencies of a small market. This can reflect either a lower degree of management efficiency and labour productivity (because management directly and labour indirectly are not subjected to the external discipline of the more competitive U.S. market) or technical scale effects (because of the duplication of labour tasks[34] and capital equipment involved in fragmented production runs).

There is ample evidence of technical scale effects. Instances are frequently cited of how short production runs induce frequent changeovers, idle capital, and costly inventories. Canadian manufacturers expressed the opinion that they could reduce costs in the range of 15 to 20 percent if they could operate at U.S. scale. This confirms our independent estimate of U of 17½ percent in Figure 1.[35] A further implication is that U represents restricted scale, rather than management or labour inefficiency *per se*. No one familiar with the industry will be surprised by our estimate that scale effects are the major present competitive cost problem of the Canadian industry. When furniture manufacturers (or almost any other manufacturers, for that matter) are asked why their costs are higher than in the United States, their first reply is almost invariably: "the size of the Canadian market."

Consider in detail how scale effects raise Canadian costs.

(i) *Excessive duplication of capital equipment.* While many U.S. case-goods plants increasingly concentrate on the assembly of precut subcontracted parts, the Canadian industry by and large continues to have fully integrated plants. Each plant has its own breakout department (for preliminary cutting), kilns (for drying the wood), and dimension stock shops

[33]Quarterly financial reports of corporations, Federal Trade Commission.

[34]Since the restricted Canadian market prevents the efficient allocation of labour (and capital), observed labour productivity in Canada will be lower. This follows even though the Canadian labour force is inherently as productive—i.e., even though a Canadian worker performs any given task equally efficiently. Cf., the discussion in 2B above.

[35]Since U could not be estimated directly, it had to be estimated as the residual left unexplained after all other influences were accounted for. The major problem in this sort of estimating technique is that all errors in prior estimates accumulate in U. This, however, is not as serious a problem as it sounds. If errors in prior estimates are randomly distributed with a mean of zero, they will tend to be self-cancelling—i.e., there will be no bias in the estimating procedure.

Curiously, our estimate of U is almost exactly equal to our estimate of the higher Canadian price (P). There is no analytical reason for expecting this; as far as one can judge, it is pure coincidence.

(for final cutting to specific dimensions). In the bedding industry the situation is similar. Several intermediate-size firms have their own coilers even though their volume of sales does not warrant such an investment. Similarly, chrome-furniture manufacturers often bend their own steel (and in some instances even do their own plating) rather than specialize in the assembly and marketing of prebent forms. The result is that this machinery is frequently idle.[36] When industry spokesmen were questioned on this apparently irrational investment, it was justified on the grounds that suppliers were unable to provide components of the desired degree of "quality." This is a simple variation on an earlier theme: components of equal quality cost more in Canada. This suggests that the Canadian tariff structure may protect inefficient scale in supplying industries.

(ii) Research, design and development. Sales in Canada are not large enough for many firms to support these overhead expenditures. As an example, consider design. Because most Canadian firms cannot afford first-class design, various options come into play.

An extreme measure was at one time suggested for the auto industry; the large companies, it was argued, should form a consortium to produce a "Canadian car," carefully designed to service the northern climate and to satisfy Canadian tastes. The Canadian market, the argument went, would be sufficient to allow the industry to achieve full economies of scale and hence price at internationally competitive levels. The intractable problems posed by such an auto scheme would be even more pronounced in furniture. The large number of furniture firms would increase the difficulties of arriving at a consortium agreement. Further, if an agreement were feasible, a monopoly-like concentration would result, with little assurance that efficiency gains would go to the consumer and not to the industry.

The big problem, however, is one of taste. Even though a dining-room suite may be a masterpiece of design and craftsmanship, it will be resisted by a consumer if every third house in his neighbourhood—and in the country—sports an identical suite. (Even if consumers could be induced into large-scale purchases, it is hard to justify this type of policy on aesthetic grounds.) As consumers able to afford variety turned to imports, the large Canadian markets (on which this policy was predicated) would not materialize. Hence the industry could not afford its quality design and development, nor could it reduce price by longer runs. The argument that the Canadian market is large enough to support one or a few producers of optimum scale is insufficient. In such a taste item as furniture, economies of scale can be achieved only in a market many times the optimal level of output of a single firm.

[36]The Department of Industry encourages the use of dimension stock and precut or bent components, but the industry has been slow to change.

The present situation of the industry is almost at the other extreme, with a proliferation of inexpensive designs produced for a fragmented Canadian market. To keep design costs at a minimum, pieces are often copied from U.S. furniture shows. The design is, of course, modified slightly.[37] In the process the Canadian manufacturer often bows to market pressure by adding a feature to attract an entirely new group of consumers. The result is not always a happy one. As one manufacturer said in a candid moment, "Usually we copy an American design and somehow manage to foul it up slightly." The problem is not bad taste; this is simply the reaction of a producer cornered in a limited market who attempts to cater to widely divergent tastes. In these circumstances, economic success is often aesthetic disaster.

(iii) Economies of scale in distribution. Canadian manufacturers are often restricted in their marketing methods by the small domestic market. All but the largest firms rely on commission salesmen. These salesmen are normally paid a retainer plus commission—or commission only—and often represent four or five firms. As a consequence, they may be unable to do full justice to the products of each firm. Furthermore, the Canadian market is not only small; it is also spread out over space. The long distance between factory and outlying population makes it difficult and expensive to adequately service lines in terms of inventory, repairs, etc. A further complication is the lengthy delay in delivery. Manufacturers typically defer cutting a piece until sufficient orders are on hand to justify the necessary changeover. Because of their shortage of liquid capital, most producers are unwilling to cut and make up items in anticipation of orders. (There are, however, a few exceptions in Quebec.) Another distribution problem in a limited market is illustrated in a rule of thumb used by the industry: once a firm reaches 12 percent of the market in a particular type of furniture, it must diversify its lines in order to enlist additional retail outlets.

(iv) Obsolete plant and equipment. It is difficult to analyze the problem of obsolescence, since it is almost certainly both a cause and an effect of higher Canadian costs. Many firms continue to manufacture in plants long since outdated, using machinery long since obsolete; as a consequence their costs are higher. The ancient buildings with poor production layout are wasteful of time and capital. With a few exceptions, the case-goods industry continues to use inefficient plants in rural areas that were once close to the forests but are now far from both timber supplies and markets.

But why does the industry not modernize and relocate? At least part of the answer is the difficulty of raising funds, because of the problems the

[37]Many U.S. firms also design in this way. And it must be recognized that it is exceedingly difficult to draw a line between copies and designs that are original. For example, are any of the "new" French Provincial designs original?

industry faces. Thus the higher costs of the industry (discussed above) become a cause (as well as an effect) of continued obsolescence.

3. *An unanswered question: Why have not economies of scale induced industry nationalization?*

Since economies of scale are the major explanation of higher Canadian cost, why do not large firms expand, in the process reducing costs and eliminating competition? A Canadian firm might expand by capturing a larger share of the domestic market and/or by exploiting export markets.

A. WHY HAVE FIRMS NOT EXPANDED IN THE DOMESTIC CANADIAN MARKET? Manufacturers are of the opinion that available economies of scale can be achieved in case goods or upholstery by a firm with an output of $15–$20 million per year. (Such a firm would have a separate breakout and dimension plant, one plant for chairs, one for case goods, one for occasional pieces, and one for upholstered goods. It would be able to centralize bookkeeping and maintain its own sales force.)[38]

It is evident that the Canadian market is sufficiently large[39] to support several case-goods firms of this optimum size. Instead, there are over two thousand establishments, with the output of the largest limited to the $6 million range. Expansion of firms in the Canadian market has been deterred for two reasons.

First, competitive pressures have not been allowed to operate to squeeze out the inefficient. Special government programs (tax concessions, loans, etc.) have helped not only the efficient but also the inefficient. Even more important is the Canadian tariff, which has provided a price cover for furniture firms. While there is no evidence that the higher Canadian price has allowed higher Canadian profits, it has allowed continuing higher costs. But the nagging question remains: why has one farsighted Canadian manager not seized the initiative and, by increasing volume, reduced cost and price?

Once again, the answer is that furniture is a taste item. And consumers prefer variety to lower cost. This is the critical trade-off. Industry spokesmen recognize that a large Canadian firm ($6 million sales) could decrease its costs and prices by 15 to 20 percent by increasing its output to three to

---

[38]Estimates of optimal bedding plants varied greatly but ranged around a figure of $1 million in sales per year. Such an operation would include coilers, garneters, etc.
[39]Canadian sales of domestic case goods in 1962 were $126 million.

five times its present level.[40] This policy is not undertaken, because this price reduction would be insufficient to attract such a large increase in sales.

B. WHY NOT EXPANSION BASED ON EXPORT SALES?

Because of its proximity, the United States provides by far the most promising export market. Even a limited probe into this market would greatly increase Canadian output and provide scale economies. But Canadian firms have not been able to market there at an attractive enough price. Even if full economies of scale were to be achieved by an expanding Canadian firm, its potential cost reduction ($U = 17\frac{1}{2}$ percent in Figure 1) would allow a reduction in its prices only to about the U.S. factory price level.[41] Even assuming that it could overcome initial design and distribution difficulties, the Canadian industry would be barely competitive.[42] In a tariff-ridden world this is not sufficient. Sales in the United States have been blocked by the 10 percent U.S. import duty[43] on wooden furniture and 35 percent on upholstered furniture.[44] There are also non-tariff barriers such as labelling requirements or "inspections" which involve slashing open a mattress to discover its contents.

In summary, there are two major reasons Canadian firms have not expanded to optimal scale. The domestic market is too small, given consumer preference for variety over price, and export markets have been blocked by foreign protection.

[40]I.e., we were told that a fully integrated firm could achieve full economies of scale at $20–$30 million sales (see above). Industry spokesmen estimate that this would involve a cost reduction of 15–20 percent; our estimate (U) is $17\frac{1}{2}$ percent.

[41]I.e., reduce P in Figure 1 to almost zero.

[42]Its Canadian advantages (lower wages, etc.) would be dissipated by the higher cost of protected inputs. An additional problem for the furniture industry is that protection results in less style selection of inputs as well as higher input prices. Thus Canadian upholstered furniture often fails to offer either competitive quality or range of fabric covers. As one manufacturer said, "I can beat my U.S. counterpart on price all the way up to the cover, then I really am forced to step aside."

[43]10 percent is the U.S. MFN rate for all items except chairs and metal furniture, which have a 17 percent rate.

[44]Another possibility would be for Canadian firms to sell in Canada at the high current Canadian prices, and achieve scale by selling in the United States at the domestic U.S. price (and hence absorb the U.S. tariff). It is not clear that this would be economical, even in competition with Illinois; and it will be evident in the next section that meeting North Carolina competition would be even more difficult. An added important factor is that Canadian firms would become vulnerable to U.S. anti-dumping regulations. Hence the greater their success in invading the U.S. market, the more likely would be retaliation. For an extended discussion of the economics of double pricing, see Wonnacott and Wonnacott, *Free Trade*, chaps. XIII and XV.

3. Prospects under North American Free Trade

If Canadian and U.S. tariffs on all manufactured goods were to be abolished, many of the higher costs of production in Canada would be eliminated. We now turn to the even more critical question: "Would the Canadian industry be eliminated?"

To answer this, it is necessary to consider explicitly whether free trade would allow Canadian cost reductions to competitive U.S. levels. Higher Canadian input costs due to protection (D_m and C_d) would automatically and immediately disappear. Nor could higher Canadian costs due to the restricted market (U) continue. It is evident from Figure 1 that a Canadian industry burdened by higher costs of this kind simply could not compete with low-priced imports entering duty-free from the United States. The continued existence of the Canadian industry, therefore, would require the elimination of inefficiency by scaling up to levels appropriate to the North American market.[1]

One barrier to past Canadian rationalization (i.e., the U.S. tariff) would be removed; thus duty-free access to the U.S. market would provide an incentive for Canadian rationalization. But this is not the *only* necessary incentive. In addition, Canada must be a low-cost location for furniture production; otherwise the Canadian industry will exercise its other option, i.e., close down.

An examination of the estimates below the base line in Figure 1 indicates that, given industry rationalization, Ontario manufacturers could indeed compete with those in the U.S. East North Central area. The relevant information is reproduced in the upper left-hand corner of Figure 2. Canadian free trade cost advantages W and T_m are again measured below a U.S. price/cost baseline. The Canadian cost disadvantages that would continue under free trade (C_t and C_i) are appropriately deducted in column 2, leaving the potential net free trade advantage for a fully rationalized Canadian industry (A).[2]

---

[1]Although Canadian producers would initially enjoy a wage advantage, it is not clear that this would persist in the long run. This issue is analyzed later.
[2]Recall that such an industry need no longer incur higher costs D_m, C_d, and U.

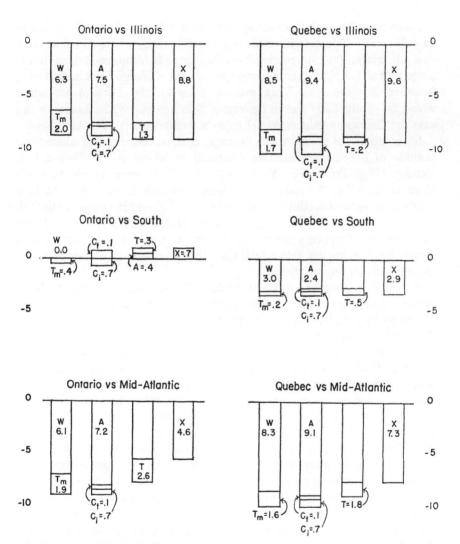

Figure 2. Comparison of Prices and Costs, 1962 (percentage by which prices and costs in Canadian region exceed those in U.S. region)

There is one other cost estimate required in evaluating the Canadian competitive position—i.e., the cost involved in shipping final products to North American markets. Since furniture markets are in population and income centres, they are concentrated in the United States. It does not follow, however, that Canadian producers are at a disadvantage. For example, in shipping furniture to the largest market (New York City),

Toronto firms enjoy an advantage (T) over Chicago firms equivalent to an estimated 1.3 percent of total costs.[3] In column 3, this is added to other cost advantages (A); in combination they provide furniture-makers in Toronto with an 8.8 percent cost advantage (X) over Chicago firms in delivering furniture into the New York market. (Clearly, the Toronto advantage would be substantially less in delivering furniture to, say, St. Louis; in this case the Chicago producer would enjoy a transport-cost advantage.)

Six comparisons are shown in Figure 2, each representing the competitive position of a Canadian location (Toronto or Montreal) vis-à-vis a U.S. location (High Point, New York, or Chicago).[4] In terms of potential free trade costs, either Toronto or Montreal compares favourably with U.S. locations in the north. But the picture is quite different in comparisons with the U.S. South; Ontario costs would be at least as high as in North Carolina, and Quebec costs would be only slightly lower. A key issue is clearly the U.S. region with which Canadian producers must compete; and this depends on product line.

It is now appropriate to consider the different impacts of free trade on various product groupings. It will be evident from the discussion below that prospects vary widely among the four sectors into which we have divided the industry. Nor does variation end there. Even *within* any of these sectors (e.g., case-goods), some subsectors would fare better than others. Indeed, because of differences in management energy and outlook, one might expect a differential effect of free trade even at the firm level; that is, the impact may vary widely among firms engaged in precisely the same furniture-making activity. This is not an argument against the average cost figures presented in this study or against the broad conclusions inferred from them; these have been necessary to give an over-all picture of the competitive strength of the industry. It is simply a warning that these figures cannot be uncritically applied to all activities nor to all Canadian furniture firms. Our only observation is that these estimates are, to our knowledge, unbiased; that is, one may expect a roughly equal distribution of firms in a weaker competitive position *and* in a stronger position than our averages imply. Canadian specialization will be concentrated in the latter group. With this

[3]The differential was calculated in the same way as shown in chap. 2, n. 17. The market centre was taken as New York City, and the distances from that city to the points of production were calculated; in each case the difference between each of the Canadian and American centres was found. This was then multiplied by the cost of shipping furniture per dollar mile times the total output of furniture. The resulting product was in turn divided by the total output of furniture shipped in Canada and expressed as a fraction.

[4]Note that in the bottom two comparisons, T is negative—i.e., either Canadian location faces a transport-cost disadvantage vis-à-vis the U.S. Mid-Atlantic region in delivering final output to New York.

caveat in mind, it is now appropriate to consider how free trade might affect the four major sectors of the furniture industry.

1. *Local cabinet shops*

Regardless of the exact nature of the trade agreement, the portion of the industry devoted to local or custom work will be relatively unaffected.[5] These small cabinet shops typically employ fourteen persons or less and manufacture furniture to order. They number slightly more than one-half of all the establishments listed in the annual DBS surveys and employ 8 to 10 percent of the total labour force in the industry. Regardless of how much tariffs rise or fall, or how extensive the penetration of imports, these firms are likely to continue their present operations; they will be about as immune to lower priced imports in the future as they have been to lower priced domestic factory furniture in the past.[6]

2. *Upholstery, mattresses, and bedding*

The sector of the industry with the best free trade growth prospects may well be the bedding and upholstery business. High weight/value ratios make distant shipment of these products unprofitable; hence the industry is market-oriented. As a consequence, Canadian locations would compete against northern U.S. locations, but not against locations in the U.S. South. If Canadian firms were able to develop their own designs or to manufacture American designs under licence, they should be able to survive; they might even expand through sales in urban markets along the border. It is evident from the Canadian/U.S. North comparisons in Figure 2 that lower wages would allow an efficient Canadian manufacturer near the border to produce and distribute his product across the line in the United States at a lower cost than that of his U.S. counterpart.[7] Moreover, since this is the most labour-intensive segment of the industry, its wage advantage would be even greater than the average estimates for the industry shown in Figure 2. Hence, there seems to be an incentive for the reorganization and scaling up of Canadian facilities to exploit these border markets.

It would be only in the very highest-priced lines, where exclusive designs

[5]Except in a city such as Windsor, which is part of the same metropolitan area as Detroit.
[6]Any reduction in their sales is more likely to come from the increased variety of available imports, rather than from their lower prices.
[7]Provided there is free trade in all manufactured goods. If free trade is limited to furniture, higher input costs (D_m) would erode this Canadian advantage.

and fabrics are essential, that Canadian firms might be unable to compete. Here production costs are of second-order importance, and a marginal advantage for Canada of this kind might not provide sufficient incentive to overcome major design problems. In any case, it is not clear that continental markets would be able to support more than the several firms of this type already existing in the United States. Rather it is in the lower-priced lines of upholstered furniture and bedding that the Canadian industry will have the greatest chance for survival, and perhaps even expansion.

3. *Case goods*

This is the most vulnerable Canadian sector because it *does* have to face southern competition. Relatively low weight/value ratios make case-goods profitable to ship longer distances. This, along with substantial economies of scale, has resulted in spatial concentration of the U.S. industry in the low-wage South. Under free trade, southern case-goods producers would be able to sell in Canadian markets on roughly the same terms that they now sell in the U.S. North. Could Canadian producers meet this competition?

A. INCENTIVE FOR REORGANIZATION
From Figure 2, it is evident that Canadian producers—especially in Ontario—would have little incentive for rationalizing their production. Their costs would not be substantially lower than in the U.S. South because, unlike most Canadian industries, they would enjoy no wage advantage. It is quite true that any efficient Canadian firms now geared up to hit U.S. markets with distinctive designs and quality workmanship should be in a reasonably competitive position because of rough potential equality with southern costs. But Canadian firms embedded in the inefficiencies of the traditional Canadian market would need to change rapidly or face deep trouble. Furthermore, it is not clear that there would be a great incentive for them to embark on a program of change. From Figure 2, it is evident that they could hope for little cost advantage, even after they completed a rationalization program; and during the interim overhaul period, they would face substantial once-and-for-all adjustment costs and problems.

B. PROBLEMS OF ADJUSTMENT
(*a*) *Rising wage rates.* Our analysis of comparative costs is based on the assumption that Canadian wage rates remain in their present position relative to U.S. rates. But across-the-board free trade is likely to change

relative wages. The general equilibrium effects of free trade have been analyzed elsewhere;[8] if expected general equilibrium pressures materialize, the Canadian dollar would appreciate towards parity with the U.S. dollar,[9] and/or the Canadian wage level would shift up towards the U.S. level. The problem is not that furniture wages in Canada would rise towards U.S. levels (they are already at par with the U.S. South); rather, the difficulty is that a possible appreciation of wages in other areas of Canadian manufacturing may tend to attract the labour force out of furniture. Given the present equality of costs in Canada and the U.S. South, it is not clear that Canadian case-goods manufacturers could retain their labour force by matching upward shifts in wages in other Canadian sectors. The major consolation is that shifts within the U.S. wage structure are likely to occur at the same time. Thus, wages in the U.S. South are likely to continue to close on the U.S. average; and in particular furniture wages in North Carolina may come under upward pressure with increased concentration of the industry there.

(b) *Problems of industry structure, finance, marketing, and design.* The average Canadian firm with sales in the $1–$3 million range would face other major difficulties. Typically it operates in a building some fifty years of age, producing a limited line of well-built pieces selling in the middle- to upper-price range. It is family-owned and suffers from undercapitalization and lack of trained engineering skills. It has a sales force working on commission and no established line of access into the U.S. market. Such a firm, lacking originality of design, with extended delivery dates, and with limited ability to extend finance to dealers, would be exceedingly vulnerable to competition from the giant U.S. firms. Unfortunately, it is these firms, often located in small towns where they are the most important employer, that do the bulk of the business and employ a major portion of the labour force in the industry.

Structural detail on the industry is shown in Table VIII. The major portion of business (92 percent) is done by incorporated companies. Moreover, Canadian ownership dominates the industry: privately owned Canadian firms account for almost 70 percent of total sales, while U.S. subsidiaries account for only about 10 percent.

Note from Table IX that U.S. subsidiaries are spread throughout the industry, while U.S.-licensed firms are mainly concentrated in bedding. The most plausible explanation is that brand identification is greater in bedding than in any other sector of the furniture industry; thus the major advantage

---

[8]Wonnacott and Wonnacott, *Free Trade*, chap. XI.
[9]Because our wage comparisons have been in terms of domestic dollars, this parity assumption has already been built into our comparative cost analysis.

TABLE VIII

STRUCTURAL CHARACTERISTICS OF THE CANADIAN FURNITURE INDUSTRY

Type of ownership	Establishments	Value of shipments	Percentage of total value shipped
		($000)	
Individual	1,007	23,450	5.1
Partnership	196	12,870	2.8
Incorporated companies:	837	425,880	92.1
U.S. subsidiaries	18	47,500*	10.2
U.S. licensed	16	22,000*	4.8
Canadian public companies	19	41,000	8.9
Canadian private companies	784	315,380	68.2

Sources: DBS, *Miscellaneous Furniture Industries*, 1963, *Office Furniture Industry*, 1963, *Household Furniture Industry*, 1963, and Department of Industry work sheet.
   *Estimates.

TABLE IX

BREAKDOWN OF FURNITURE-MAKING ACTIVITIES
IN EACH OWNERSHIP CLASSIFICATION
(percentages)

	Bedding	Metal office	Uphol-stered	Comm. cabinets	Wooden household	Miscel-laneous
U.S. subsidiaries	24.8	22.8	21.3	16.8	11.7	2.6
U.S. licensed	95.0		5.0			
Canadian public companies		37.9	2.6	23.2	28.9	7.5

Sources: DBS, *Miscellaneous Furniture Industries*, 1963, *Office Furniture Industry*, 1963, *Household Furniture Industry*, 1963, and Department of Industry work sheet.

of association with a U.S. firm is acquiring its well-known brand name. To do this, a Canadian firm requires only a licensing agreement.

While the cost equality in Figure 2 suggests little incentive for firms of this kind to reorganize, it also implies that Canadian firms which are already at, or near, U.S. efficiency levels should be in a competitive position. In addition to matching production costs, there will be other tests of survival: quality design and the ability to market aggressively in the United States as Canadian sales are lost to imports. These two problems are interrelated and may require imaginative solutions. For example, a Canadian firm may seek a custom contract with a large U.S. department store (or chain) to produce a quality line to its design specifications. Such a contract might cover the interim period of adjustment of the firm and provide it with a breathing spell in which to plan a broader attack on U.S.

markets by independent sale of its own designs. Canadian firms correctly recognize that, even if they can compete in terms of price in Canadian markets with U.S. imports, they may still lose sales as consumers exercise choice over a greater variety of (imported) designs. Hence, even if they can effectively compete in the North American market, they will tend to lose sales in Canada. But it is important to recognize that this argument cuts both ways. A Canadian firm need carve only a very small segment out of the vast U.S. market to more than compensate for its loss of Canadian sales; and the more attractive and unique its design, the more will its segment of the market be insulated from price competition. In such a taste item as furniture, quality design and craftsmanship may provide the "protection" in the North American market in the future that tariffs have provided in the Canadian market in the past. Developing tasteful and unique designs is no simple matter. For example, the "Swedish modern" designs characteristic of Scandinavian furniture were not developed overnight, but only after a prolonged process of trial and error extending over a period of ten to thirty years.

In any circumstances, the disciplines of a broader, more competitive market yield substantial benefits, both for consumers facing more attractive prices and for labour and management receiving higher rewards for efficiency. Competition, however, involves a cost as well, albeit temporary: the inefficient must find work elsewhere. Tariff elimination would provide the sudden equivalent to many years of competitive change. Because Canadian firms now operate well below optimum scale, survival would require expansion; those unwilling to seize the new opportunities for expanding sales in the United States are almost certain not to survive.

It is extremely difficult to predict resulting patterns. The authors' tentative view is that a large number of privately incorporated Canadian case-goods firms would cease to exist in their present form; many would be merged with more efficient, expanding Canadian firms or U.S. firms; and the present trend of the elimination of obsolete Canadian furniture firms would be greatly accelerated. This would be offset, at least in part, by the expansion of the more efficient Canadian firms. It is not possible to estimate the combined effects of these cross forces on Canadian furniture employment. However, the complete elimination of case-goods production in Canada seems vastly too pessimistic a prediction; on the other hand, continued Canadian employment at present levels in case goods[10] seems an overly optimistic view.

[10]With increased efficiency and productivity, this implies an increase in Canadian production, both in absolute terms and relative to production in the United States. A more modest target for the industry, therefore, would be to maintain its share of North American production.

4. Special products

It is likely that there would be an equally severe adjustment problem in metal furniture. The market for dinette suites is characterized not so much by price competition as by originality of fabrics and design and increasingly complex production techniques. This sector of the industry would attach less importance to low Canadian wages, but more importance to high prevailing Canadian capital costs.[11] An advantage accruing to Canadian producers of inexpensive items is that they may be partially protected by distance, since the value/weight ratio of these finished products is low. Hence, assembly plants may continue in the major urban markets of Toronto, Montreal, and Vancouver. In inexpensive lines, these Canadian cities may have wages sufficiently below those of the U.S. North to allow them to assemble products for distribution to nearby American markets.

5. Summary of the sectoral impact of free trade

The Canadian furniture industry would face special problems not faced by many other Canadian industries.

The most mobile segment of the U.S. industry (case-goods) that might otherwise find low Canadian wages an attraction has already gone (or is in the process of going) to the equally low-wage U.S. South. Moreover, the sunk capital of an established industry in Canada would provide little insurance that the industry would continue here, since it is at present ill-adapted to the new set of circumstances. Since most firms have limited themselves to the small Canadian market, they are unprepared both for meeting import competition and for seizing market opportunities in the United States. On the other hand, there is no reason why Canadian firms that are prepared to reorganize and expose themselves to the cut and thrust of international competition cannot expand on the basis of increased U.S. sales. Adjustment of the industry would be easier if the initial free trade period is one of rapid over-all economic growth.

Continued existence of custom work in Canada and (to a lesser degree) of upholstery and bedding is to be expected because of the localized or semi-localized nature of the product. On the same grounds there are good prospects for the assembly of relatively inexpensive lines of metal furniture in Canada.

---

[11]This is especially true of stamped metal furniture. Similar difficulties would be involved in the production of institutional items (e.g., hospital beds) which are also capital-intensive.

4. Implications of a
North Atlantic Free Trade Area

If North American free trade were extended to include Europe and Japan, case goods would be the only furniture items substantially affected. Even in such a broader free trade area, the survival of the Canadian industry would remain contingent on its ability to face competition with U.S. producers in North American markets. Therefore, Canada's prospects under North Atlantic free trade must be projected from the best available estimate of the outcome of Canadian competition with the United States. Specifically, we must consider the two extreme limits (defined in chap. 3, section 3) within which North American adjustment is almost certain to fall: the far too pessimistic view that Canadians will be totally unable to compete with U.S. case-goods manufacturers and the Canadian industry will disappear; and the (probably) overoptimistic assumption that the Canadian case-goods industry could succeed in retaining its present share of North American employment. The implications of these two extremes will now be examined in turn.

1. *An extreme case: The demise of the Canadian case-goods industry and the pattern of increased imports*

Canadian producers unable to meet U.S. competition in Canada can hardly be expected to compete in third markets. With the decline of Canadian case-goods production, North Atlantic trade patterns would be determined by competition between European and U.S. producers. In these circumstances, the only major question for Canada becomes the pattern of case-goods imports. These would increase for two reasons: first, to displace domestic Canadian production and, second, to satisfy increased demand in Canada induced by lower prices and greater style selection. In this (admittedly unrealistic) set of limiting circumstances, case-goods imports would increase by many times their present level.

Where would these imports originate? U.S. producers would be likely to capture the lion's share of new Canadian imports for several reasons: geographic proximity, low transport costs, and style preferences in Canada induced by U.S. advertising. However, U.S. producers are unlikely to corner this market. For one thing, European competitors would enjoy a substantial wage advantage; European success in Canadian markets seems most likely in handmade lines, which allow maximum exploitation of this advantage. (The European transport-cost disadvantage would also be less critical in these expensive lines.) In such expensive items, style becomes a critical factor. The European ability to exploit (and induce) taste changes in North America is likely to be the key issue—especially because rising U.S. and Canadian incomes will allow indulgence in wide swings in taste. This argument, of course, cuts both ways: style and taste variations in Europe may also be exploited by U.S. producers.

Given the pessimistic assumptions of this section, the effects of free trade can be sketched out. For reasons of both price and style, U.S./European trade (in both directions) would increase with free trade. Both U.S. and European producers would increase sales in Canada, displacing Canadian production; but it seems likely that U.S. manufacturers would capture the larger portion of these markets.

2. *The other extreme: Suppose a rationalized Canadian case-goods industry retains its present share of North American employment*

In this more complicated case, three effects must be considered. The first two follow from the elimination of U.S. and Canadian tariffs only, regardless of whether or not Europe cooperates; the third is the additional effect of tariff removal between Europe and North America.

A. THE EFFECTS OF CANADIAN/U.S. TARIFF REMOVAL ON
   CANADIAN/U.S. TRADE

Reciprocal tariff reductions by the two countries would result in a large, balanced[1] increase in Canadian exports to, and imports from, the United States. The rationalization of North American production implies a concurrent rationalization in consumption. To the degree that Canadian furniture-consumption patterns come anywhere near approximating those of the United States, a many-fold increase in Canadian imports from the United States would result; this follows strictly from the relative size of Canadian and U.S.[2] markets and production.

[1]This follows (approximately) from Canadian retention of present share of North American employment.
[2]U.S. furniture production now represents over 90 percent of North American consumption and would, under the circumstances here considered, continue to dominate to this degree. If Canadian consumption patterns approach those in the United States, U.S. production would satisfy over 90 percent of Canadian (as well as U.S.) con-

B. THE EFFECTS OF CANADIAN/U.S. TARIFF REMOVAL ON TRADE
WITH THIRD COUNTRIES

Successful rationalization implies substantial Canadian cost reductions. Hence Canadian producers would be able to compete more effectively with third-country producers in third-country markets and *also* in Canada. This suggests an increase in Canadian exports to third countries and a reduction in Canadian imports from these areas.

It is extremely difficult to predict the size of these increased trade flows. The only benchmark of any kind available is present U.S. performance vis-à-vis third countries. Canadian cost reduction to U.S. levels not only implies the ability to compete on equal terms with U.S. producers in North America; it should also imply the ability to match U.S. competition in third markets.[3] Thus, in competing in third countries, Canadian producers would face the same advantages and disadvantages U.S. producers now face.

Multilateral trading patterns are shown in Table X. It is not surprising that U.S. trade with third countries greatly exceeds Canadian trade with third countries, given the relative size of Canada and the United States. This table is more useful in pointing up the stronger competitive position in third markets of the present (lower-cost) U.S. industry: U.S. exports to third countries are roughly 65 percent of imports, but the equivalent export/import fraction for Canada is just over 25 percent. To the extent that reduced free trade costs would allow Canadian producers to emulate U.S. performance vis-à-vis third countries, increased Canadian exports to third countries and decreased Canadian imports from third countries should tend to increase the Canadian export/import fraction towards the U.S. level. Canadian trade would be unlikely to reach this level, since, at best, U.S. performance is only a long-run benchmark guide. But even if this trend did run its full course, the resulting changes in Canadian trade flows would not compare in magnitude with the potential changes considered in section A above.

---

sumption. This implies that Canadian imports from the United States would grow from their present level of less than 10 percent to over 90 percent of Canadian consumption. (Imports would grow not only from this structural change, but also because of normal market growth and the growth in Canadian sales induced by lower prices. A similar growth in exports implies that Canadian producers would be selling about 90 percent of their output in the United States.)

No one would predict this sort of change. Even under free trade, and even considering only the most mobile product (case goods), consumption patterns in the two countries would be unlikely to conform to this degree. Instead, a producer in either country would likely capture a larger proportion of domestic than of foreign markets. But even conceding this, the rationalization of consumption is likely to increase Canadian imports by many times their current levels, and (smaller present) Canadian exports by an even greater multiple.

[3] A difficulty arises in cases where Canadian and U.S. exporters do not face similar tariffs by third countries. This issue is dealt with below in n. 5.

C. EFFECTS OF TARIFF ELIMINATION BETWEEN NORTH AMERICA AND EUROPE

Since the effects of tariff elimination between Canada and the United States have been traced out in A and B, it is now appropriate to turn to the further effects of free trade between North America and Europe. M. E. Kreinin's estimates indicate that trade flows between the United States and Europe would increase in both directions by about 50 percent as a result of free trade.[4] Similar effects on Canadian trade flows with third countries are likely.[5] Though sizable, these effects would not compare with the changes considered in A.

[4]In his not yet published manuscript, "Trade Arrangements in the Atlantic Community—Effects on the United States," he estimates 1960 trade flows, as they would have been affected by free trade, as follows:

U.S. TRADE IN FURNITURE ($ MILLION)

	1960 U.S. imports	Hypothetical increase in U.S. imports from tariff reduction	1960 U.S. exports	Hypothetical increase in U.S. exports from tariff reduction
U.S. trade with:				
AFTA (Atlantic Free Trade Area)*	18.9	10.0	20.0	9.0
AFTA (ex. EEC)	13.4	7.1	19.1	8.8

*Includes the EEC, EFTA, Canada, and Japan.

A comparison of the figures in the two rows indicates that it makes some difference whether or not the EEC participates. With EEC participation, the slight present U.S. surplus of exports over imports would be reduced by free trade. On the other hand, without EEC participation the conclusion is reversed: the present U.S. surplus would be increased somewhat. In either case, however, the mix of production in the United States and Europe remains basically unaltered, with furniture trade increased in the order of 50 percent.

[5]A difficulty arises because of the different third-country tariffs now faced by Canada and the United States; e.g., Canadian participation in the Commonwealth preference system. Thus the trends examined in B should be modified to the extent that Canada and the United States would face different tariffs by these third countries. But for precisely the same reason, the estimates in (3) would require modification because the tariffs being removed against Canada and the United States would differ. But these modifications to B and C cancel out; so no conceptual problem is involved if they are ignored in both instances.

If difficulty with this argument remains, the reader may view the move to Atlantic free trade as involving two distinct stages. First, the formation of a Canada-U.S. customs union with a common external tariff set at the present U.S. level. Its effects are analyzed in A and B. Thus B becomes an estimate of the effects on Canadian third-country trade of Canadian cost reductions *and* a shift onto the U.S. tariff position vis-à-vis third countries (including Canadian exit from Commonwealth preference). The second stage is the formation of a North Atlantic free trade area by the elimination of tariffs between the North Atlantic customs union and Europe. This is estimated in section C; in this final stage Canada and the United States would enjoy equivalent tariff reductions by third countries.

TABLE X

MULTILATERAL TRADE FLOWS IN FURNITURE, 1961
(mil. $ U.S.)

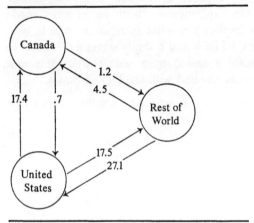

Source: U.N. *Commodity Trade Statistics, 1961.*

3. *Summary of the prospects of the case-goods industry in a North Atlantic free trade area*

It has simply not been feasible to quantify each of the effects discussed above; instead, only the likely direction and rough magnitude of changes have been defined. A fairly clear picture does, however, emerge. The key for the case-goods industry is its ability to compete with U.S. producers in North American markets. At the pessimistic extreme, if it fails completely (as in 1), then there is no prospect that it can survive by capturing third markets.[6] At this extreme, domestic consumption defines the deficit in case-goods trade, and the multiple increase in imports would be drawn largely from the United States.

At the optimistic extreme, if the industry shows sufficient competitive strength to retain its present share of North American employment (as in 2) the picture becomes more complicated; prospects can be defined only by considering the combined effects of 2A, B, and C above. The effect of B is to increase exports but decrease imports. The effect of either A or C is to increase

[6]Even Commonwealth preference would no longer afford Canadian producers any protection, since this system could hardly survive under North Atlantic free trade. (In any event, the only significant Canadian furniture exports to the Commonwealth now are to Bermuda and Trinidad, and these combined in 1961 scarcely exceeded half a million dollars.)

both exports and imports by roughly equal amounts. In sum, these imply a multiple increase in both exports and imports, with the present export-import deficit in furniture slightly reduced in absolute terms but greatly reduced in relative terms. The other question is, "With whom will Canada engage in all this new trade?" A implies a multiple increase in trade in both directions with the United States, while B and C imply increased exports to Europe.[7] Since A would dominate B and C by a wide margin, this new Canadian trade will be heavily concentrated with the United States.

[7]The effect on Canadian imports from Europe is not clear, since the influence of B and C operate in opposite directions.

5. Free Trade Benefits and Costs

1. *Effects on the Canadian consumer*

A. LOWER PRICE ON PRESENT CANADIAN PURCHASES

The major benefit of free trade would be that the Canadian consumer would pay less for all purchased furniture which is now domestically produced. (He would also pay less for imported furniture; but this would be offset by the equal burden he would bear as a taxpayer, since the import duty on furniture would no longer be collected by the Canadian government.[1]) The factory price of domestic furniture production in 1962 in Canada was $363 million; deducting exports of $3 million leaves a balance of $360 million. This domestic product would have cost Canadians an estimated 15.3 percent less[2] under free trade—or a saving of about $55 million.

B. BENEFITS ON INCREASED PURCHASES

While the above represents the benefit involved on present purchases, it must be recognized that purchases would be increased at this lower price. The benefits involved on these additional purchases[3] depend on the response of consumers to lower prices. Our statistical estimate of the price elasticity of Canadian furniture demand was substantially less than unity, which intuitively seems on the low side.[4] However, even this figure yields an estimated $2–$3 million of free trade benefits to consumers on additional

---

[1]For a clarification of this and other issues in this section, see Harry Johnson, "The Cost of Protection and the Scientific Tariff," *Journal of Political Economy*, Aug. 1960.

[2]I.e., the present Canadian price is 18 percent above the world (i.e., U.S.) price (see above, section 1A); or the world price is 15.3 percent below the present Canadian price.

[3]This is the consumer surplus triangle in Johnson, "The Cost of Protection and the Scientific Tariff."

[4]From a time series regression of (price-deflated) furniture sales on price and (price-deflated) GNP. Because this is a relatively insignificant free trade benefit, no attempt was made to improve on our single-equation, least-squares estimate by taking account of identification difficulties, etc.

furniture purchases. And if demand elasticity were to be as high as two, estimated benefits would exceed $8 million.

C. WIDER RANGE OF CHOICE

There would be an additional benefit for consumers, who would face a much wider choice. It is impossible to estimate the value the consumer would place on increased variety; but it is almost certain to fall within the range of 0–$67 million.[5] This is clearly a consideration of major importance; restricted choice *may* be more costly to Canadians than higher price.[6]

In total, therefore, the per annum benefits of free trade to the Canadian consumer are valued on a 1962 base at $57–$125 million.[7]

[5]This maximum figure is derived by estimating the cost to the consumer of exercising his option of purchasing U.S. imports instead of Canadian furniture. Because of the tariff alone, these imports would cost 25 percent more than the U.S. price. But that is not all. Additional handling and distribution charges are imposed on imported items; or the consumer who takes the trouble of shopping in the United States incurs substantial cost and inconvenience. (There also may be a problem of paying sales taxes in both countries.) The maximum figures in the third column of Table I indicate that selected Canadian items can be priced almost 40 percent above U.S. equivalents without inducing Canadians to exercise their option of purchasing in the United States. This suggests that the frictions involved provide Canadian producers with an additional 15 percent of price insulation above and beyond the 25 percent provided by the tariff.

If this U.S. price plus 40 percent is assumed to be the price at which Canadians would opt to purchase in the U.S. market, then the Canadian consumer is worse off by this same 40 percent because of protection. Of this, 18 percent reflects higher Canadian price and has already been estimated as a cash equivalent of about $55 million. The remaining 22 percent, or roughly $67 million, is our maximum estimate of the cost of restricted Canadian choice.

This is regarded as a maximum bound, since many Canadians undoubtedly place a lower valuation on variety than this estimate implies. (Note that the argument above is based on the assumption that all Canadians would behave like those who place a high premium on variety—i.e., those who would switch purchases to the United States if the Canadian price were to reach the U.S. price plus 40 percent.) However, in another sense this estimate may understate; there may be a group of Canadians for whom the cost and inconvenience of shopping in the United States exceeds 15 percent. Such individuals may accordingly place a higher valuation on variety than the 22 percent figure we have used.

[6]A very limited sample of couples who have lived in both the United States and Canada were asked, "Which do you find to be a greater disadvantage in purchasing in Canada: higher price or more restricted variety?" Husbands generally pointed to price; and wives, variety. Which set of preferences is more appropriate? Once purchased, furniture apparently provides more satisfaction to women than to men. Moreover, manufacturers typically aim their advertising at women because they feel that wives make the final selection. However, this must be regarded as a restricted exercise of choice, since it is generally within a budget restraint set by the husband. This line of enquiry clearly leads to no firm estimates; but it does support our conclusion that restricted choice may be as costly to Canadians as higher price.

[7]For two reasons, even this figure represents an underestimate. No account has been

2. Income and employment effects

Effects on income recipients in the industry depend on Canadian employment displaced by imports and on labour mobility into new occupations. Since available information is inadequate on both counts, our cost estimates will be even more tentative than our benefit figures. As in similar perplexing circumstances, we shall try at least to bracket the answer by arguing from two extreme sets of assumptions.

A. THE OPTIMISTIC CASE, WITH MINIMUM RESOURCE-TRANSFER COSTS

A completely cost-free adjustment requires that *only one* of the following two assumptions hold: either (*a*) the industry successfully rationalizes to retain its present share of North American employment or (*b*) any employment shifts into other sectors involve benefits at least equal to transfer costs.

(*a*) *If the industry does not contract.* This first possibility has already been discussed in chap. 3, section 4 above. Continued Canadian furniture employment does not imply that the industry would be frozen in its present pattern. Indeed, substantial structural and geographic shifts would almost certainly occur. In this circumstance, a costless adjustment would require that losses from sunk costs[8] and the inconvenience and cost of labour relocation be covered by the increased income benefits. The new employment of the labour force will be with surviving Canadian firms, which *ipso facto* are the most efficient. They would also be expanding. For both reasons, one might expect this shift in employment to be at a higher wage rate.

---

taken of the increase in consumer surplus that would result from increased purchases due to a greater range of choice. Even more important, no account has been taken of a whole set of benefits that might accrue to the consumer if distribution and retail margins in Canada were to be affected by free trade. In this analysis, these margins are assumed to remain constant at their present *absolute* value. But in a world of falling prices, this is the assumption that *percentage* markups rise. If percentage markups do not rise in this way, then the consumer will receive an additional benefit. And this seems almost ensured—at least in border areas—by the access of Canadians to highly competitive retail outlets in the United States, such as Detroit. To evaluate this would take us too far afield, into an analysis as extended and complicated as the one here undertaken on furniture manufacturing. Suffice to note that the estimate of the free trade benefits to the consumer is almost certainly understated in this study.

[8]In the furniture industry, sunk costs are not what one would expect. By and large they would not involve furniture factories, which in many cases were fully depreciated many years ago. Instead, the major losses would fall on the host community, which frequently looks to the furniture industry as the major, if not the only, source of employment. With any departure of the furniture industry, there might be both private sunk costs (housing) and public costs (schools, etc.). But this would depend on the ability of the community to attract new employment.

Moreover, since it is a per annum benefit, a small wage increase would offset an apparently large, once-and-for-all set of adjustment costs.

(b) *If resources are sufficiently mobile.* Even if furniture employment in Canada were to contract, a costless adjustment might still occur if labour[9] were sufficiently mobile into other industries. Costs and benefits similar to those in the previous case still apply, although with minor modification.

A psychic cost may be involved for furniture workers who have to take up new tasks.[10] On the other hand, their new wages would be higher on two counts: first, because average wages in other industries exceed those in furniture[11] and, second, because Canadian wages would be rising across the board with free trade.[12] (Recall that it is this pull on labour by other industries that would make it difficult for the furniture industry to retain its labour force.) One condition for a costless transfer in this instance is, therefore, that these new wages be high enough to offset any psychic income loss in new employment, and once-and-for-all sunk costs and transfer costs.[13]

With a costless adjustment process for any of these reasons, the net benefit of free trade would be the consumer windfall of $75–$125 million.

B. THE PESSIMISTIC CASE, WITH MAXIMUM RESOURCE-TRANSFER COSTS

The most expensive conceivable cost would be incurred if resources now in furniture were to be left permanently unemployed. This outcome would require that *both* of two extreme conditions occur: that the entire portion of the industry subjected to import competition fails; *and* that resources are permanently unemployable in other sectors. Clearly, either is so unlikely that the (necessary) combination of the two may be rejected out of hand. Nevertheless, this cost will be computed as a benchmark for evaluating potential unemployment costs of a less severe nature.

The localized output of about 30 percent of the industry (e.g., custom work) leaves only 70 percent of the industry vulnerable to import compe-

[9]Labour is used in this discussion as a proxy for the more general term "resources."
[10]This cost can, of course, be negative—i.e., workers may find they enjoy the new tasks more than the old.
[11]This transfer into more productive occupations is one of the major benefits of free trade, and one that is often overlooked. In 1962, average hourly earnings of production workers in manufacturing exceeded those in furniture by 34 cents per hour. Workers now in furniture might have increased their income by as much as $16 million per annum by transferring into a mix of alternative industries paying average wages.
[12]See Wonnacott and Wonnacott, *Free Trade*, chap. XI.
[13]For this case to hold, we require only that labour be *sufficiently* mobile to satisfy this condition of cost-benefit equality. Labour would still be employed in various sectors at differing wage rates. Hence this is far less restrictive than an assumption of "perfect" mobility.

tition. On a 1962 base, maximum lost wages are estimated at 70 percent of a total payroll of $121 million, or about $85 million—a figure which is bracketed by the estimated range of $57–$125 million of consumer benefits. Hence, the cost-benefit balance can be restated as follows: free-trade consumer benefits of $57–$125 million will exceed payroll losses unless most[14] of the present Canadian labour force engaged in import-competing furniture-making becomes permanently unemployed, with no prospect of ever again becoming employable.

Permanent payroll losses, of course, are an inadequate indicator of possible costs[15]; even so, it is difficult to see how continued protection of this industry can be justified in the light of these estimates. There seems to be no way of reasonably arguing that permanent unemployment of even, say, a quarter of the labour force would follow as a result of free trade. This would require arguing a whole set of propositions; regardless of the likelihood of any of these alone, in combination they become highly implausible. These include (1) a pessimistic view of industry prospects under free trade; (2) permanent inability of displaced labour to get alternative employment at any wage rate—a proposition which is directly contradicted by every historical precedent; and (3) a paralysis of government policy, involving the payment of staggering sums in unemployment insurance but no effective monetary or fiscal response, relocation, or retraining assistance. And anyone bold enough to argue such a case must then recognize that even though this implies that costs equal benefits initially, they cannot continue

[14]I.e., 67–100 percent.

[15]For example, equity earnings and government corporate tax receipts would be reduced in a declining industry. (These have been estimated at roughly $11 million in 1962.) Furniture-supplying industries might or might not contract their operations, depending on elasticities of domestic and foreign demand from other sources; if they were forced to contract (or reduce their prices to foreign purchasers), a cost might be involved. Finally, unemployment has familiar multiplier effects, as reduced purchases by the unemployed result in reduced sales of consumer goods, and so on. These multiplier effects could be very large if they were to apply to all lost furniture payroll. But they do not; since the unemployed would receive unemployment insurance and tax reductions, these multiplier effects would apply only to a fraction of their income loss. Even this might be offset by compensating monetary and fiscal policy.

It is not clear by how much payroll losses of the permanently unemployed might understate total costs of a declining industry. However, it is the authors' view that total costs are unlikely to exceed permanent payroll losses by more than 50–100 percent.

Except for factories that are closed down, no sunk costs are involved; the unemployed labour force would continue to use its present housing, schools, etc. Its income (unemployment insurance) is an income transfer, rather than a cost. It is assumed in this argument that workers receive the same psychic satisfaction from leisure as from building furniture. In other words, the only reason they would be less happy when unemployed would be because their income would be reduced to the unemployment insurance level.

to do so. For costs must decrease over time as the permanently unemployed "retire" from the labour force; but benefits will increase over time with the increase in Canadian consumption of furniture.

There is, of course, the non-economic argument that there is a social benefit involved in maintaining a large Canadian furniture industry—i.e., that there is some inherent advantage in having present furniture-makers continue in their present tasks, rather than turning their hands to the production of aluminum or automobiles. Since this is a value judgment rather than a conclusion following a logical chain of reasoning, it can be neither proven nor disproven.[16]

---

[16]Two other economic arguments deserve comment. The infant-industry argument can scarcely be used to support continued protection of an industry so heavily marked by age. Another conceivable justification for protection is that management, like labour, is unable to turn its hand to other activities and that furniture-supplying industries would be unable to find either alternative domestic or export markets. In other words, if one takes the view that the Canadian economy is frozen into a rigid structural pattern, then any attempt to induce a more efficient allocation of economic activity is doomed to failure. Given this view, any change (such as tariff reduction or automation) is likely to involve a net cost. While this argument cannot be contradicted logically, it may be rejected on empirical grounds; the economy is just not that rigid.

6. Policy Options

In the preceding sections, the effects on the furniture industry of across-the-board free trade have been examined. In this section, a number of alternative policy options are considered; each will be compared with free trade (i.e., unrestricted, across-the-board tariff elimination), on the one hand, and present protection, on the other.

1. *A negotiated reduction of present MFN rates by one-quarter to one-third*

A. CONSUMPTION EFFECTS

With a one-quarter to one-third reduction in the present 25 percent Canadian tariff, the price of imports would fall by 6 to 8 percent. Substantial gains would go to the consumer because his present import purchases would cost less. However, this does not represent a "social gain," since it would just be offset by an equivalent loss in duty revenue to the government.[1] The net gains to the consumer/taxpayer, therefore, would come from the purchases he now directs at domestically produced furniture. If price reductions are forced upon domestic producers by lower-cost imports, the Canadian consumer benefits as a consequence. Even if Canadian producers do not lower their prices, the Canadian consumer still stands to gain; additional U.S. imports will result, and the Canadian consumer will select from a greater variety of imported items, all more attractively priced than in the past.

B. PRODUCTION EFFECTS

A reduction in the 25 percent Canadian tariff to about 17–19 percent would seriously threaten the Canadian industry in its own domestic market, since the price of landed imports would be reduced to the present level of domestically produced items.[2] If Canadian producers maintained present

[1]This "loss" is involved even though total government tariff receipts may not fall. Duty receipts from additional imports induced by the tariff reduction may offset the duty reduction on present imports.
[2]Recall that Canadian price was estimated in chap. 2, sect. 2, as about 18 percent above the U.S. price. Any error in this estimate becomes critical in evaluating the

prices, they would lose whatever small price advantage they now enjoy and hence would lose a portion of their markets to imports. Alternatively, Canadian producers attempting to maintain their competitive edge by matching this price reduction would find their profits reduced. The prospect for domestic producers is therefore bleak, unless they could use the U.S. tariff reduction to exploit new export markets.

There is little prospect that the U.S. tariff cut would allow the Canadian industry to capture sizable markets in the United States. At best, a fully rationalized, high-volume Canadian industry could produce at costs only roughly equal to those prevailing in the United States, but Canadian producers would still face a competitive disadvantage in the form of a 6 to 8 percent U.S. duty.[3] There is therefore little prospect that the industry could make up for its domestic losses in increased exports. And without wider markets, volume efficiencies could not be achieved.

C. EVALUATION

As far as the furniture industry is concerned, it is difficult to make much of an economic case for the option of MFN tariff reductions. It is true that the over-all effect could be an improvement on the present (protection) situation, but this is not a clear case and would depend on how consumer benefits might trade off against production problems. It is clear, however, that this MFN option is inferior to free trade. This is true from the point of view of the consumer, who would get less price reduction and variety from the more modest MFN cuts. It is also true from the point of view of the producer, who would face increased import competition without compensating advantages of improved access to the U.S. market.

There are two general observations that apply in any comparison of complete free trade and partial MFN tariff reductions. There may be political advantages in working towards free trade via reciprocal MFN reductions. Politicians may view a gradual program as easier to sell than a once-and-for-all dismantling of tariffs.[4] On the other hand, it is unlikely that such a process is the most efficient route to free trade. Even if one could assume that tariffs could be completely eliminated by a set of such bargaining rounds (and this is an extremely optimistic view), Canadian

---

effects of a one-quarter to one-third MFN tariff cut: if Canadian price is less (more) than our estimate, then Canadian producers will be in a stronger (weaker) position to meet import competition as a consequence.

[3]I.e., the present 10 percent rate less the one-quarter to one-third cut.

[4]It is generally assumed that Canadian industry would prefer gradual tariff reductions. However, the view of industry leaders is by no means unanimous—for the reasons cited below.

industry would become involved in a whole series of reorganizations. Thus, even if a situation of optimal efficiency is eventually reached, the path leading to it would involve needless cost. Above all, any industry rationalizing its operations by shifting from a domestic to an international base requires stable expectations of future export markets. Yet a series of MFN reductions would involve a large element of uncertainty about the eventual outcome—as well as the outcome of each particular bargaining round. And this uncertainty alone might prevent industry rationalization.

These considerations are important for any industry, but they are critical for furniture. Even if the industry were to be viable in Canada after complete tariff elimination, it may not survive the first step (i.e., the one-quarter to one-third tariff reduction) in a staged process. Furniture seems to be a marginal industry in any case; and its situation would be likely to get worse in any staging process before it got better. It must be remembered that the existence of many industries in their present locations depends heavily on inertia. If inertia is at all important in furniture-making, the contraction of this marginal industry at any point in a staging process might be irreversible.

2. Single-industry free trade

Unrestricted free trade for a single industry would allow anyone and everyone to move the product across the border duty-free; the precedent is farm implements. This is not to be confused with the limited free trade scheme in autos (discussed in the next section), which involves a number of restrictions designed to guarantee continued Canadian employment.

Unrestricted free trade in furniture would have similar effects to negotiated MFN tariff reductions. The major difference would be one of degree; the single-industry scheme would have a far greater impact on both consumers and producers.

A. CONSUMPTION EFFECTS
Consumers would enjoy maximum benefits. The free entry of imports would drive furniture prices down to the U.S. level; at the same time the consumer would enjoy the full benefits of variety provided by free access to U.S. lines.

B. PRODUCTION EFFECTS
With present techniques and volume, Canadian manufacturers would be unable to meet competition from imports; the elimination of the 25 percent

Canadian duty would leave Canadian producers at an approximate 18 percent price disadvantage vis-à-vis imports, rather than the 7 percent advantage they now enjoy.

The one hope of the industry would be to increase volume (by selling in the United States) and thus decrease costs. The most favourably situated firms might succeed; however, our aggregate figures for the industry do not indicate that rationalization of production in Canada would be profitable for the average firm in Canada. Figure 2 suggests that Canadian producers could maintain costs roughly competitive with those in North Carolina in an all-industry free trade area; but in a single-industry scheme Canadian furniture-makers would be at a substantial competitive disadvantage because of their higher cost of protected inputs. (On average, Canadian furniture costs could be almost 8 percent higher for this reason alone.)[5] This is critical in upholstered goods, since an important protected input is textiles.

The outlook for Canadian producers in such a scheme is not promising. They would face the full force of foreign competition in domestic markets. However, there would be little offsetting advantage provided by duty-free access into U.S. markets; Canadian costs would remain higher because of the protection left on other industries.

C. EVALUATION

Any comparison of such a scheme with present protection is difficult. On the one hand, Canadian consumers would enjoy maximum benefits from price reductions and increased variety. On the other hand, this scheme would involve maximum pressure on Canadian producers, and it is unlikely that most of the industry would survive. It is not clear how consumption advantages and production disadvantages would trade off. Any firm conclusion would require a cost/benefit calculation similar to that undertaken in chapter 5. And conclusions would be more difficult to reach. In this case, it would no longer be clear that benefits exceed costs by a wide margin; hence, a number of difficult issues would require clarification—e.g., how permanently displaced labour might remain unemployed and how quickly present suppliers of furniture inputs might develop alternative markets in other industries and countries.

Hence it cannot be concluded that such a scheme is superior or inferior

[5]Canadian producers could receive a drawback on import duty for export sales. This would not reduce their input costs to the U.S. level, however, since only a portion of their inputs is imported and subject to duty remission. The large portion of their inputs is purchased from domestic producers who charge a higher price because of the protection they receive. Moreover, the industry has not taken full advantage of the drawback scheme in the past.

to present protection. However, this scheme can be rejected in comparison with across-the-board free trade. The consumer would enjoy similar benefits in either case. However, producers would be worse off in a single-industry scheme because of higher input costs; accordingly, they would face greater pressure from import competition and less prospect of compensating export sales.

D. SOME DIFFICULT ISSUES RECONSIDERED

It should be noted that there are two difficult issues that arise in an analysis of this kind. First, it is necessary to argue from the present exchange rate and from present relative wage rates—even though it is recognized that these may change with tariff reductions. Thus, for example, if an MFN tariff reduction gives rise to a general shift in Canadian wages relative to those in the United States, Canadian furniture production would become more or less attractive than this impact analysis suggests. (Indeed, as long as general equilibrium shifts of this kind are allowed to take place, they ensure that Canadian labour will be fully employed—at least in the long run.)

When wages are considered variable, conclusions for a single-industry scheme are also complicated. For example, the Canadian industry might survive the severe pressure of foreign competition by suspending wage increases, thus allowing its wages to lag further below those in the United States. The conclusions above, however, remain unaffected. This scheme is less attractive than across-the-board free trade because it would involve a continuing cost—in this case the depressed Canadian wage necessary to compensate for high input costs.

The second issue that arises is the normal presumption that labour and other factors of production are worse off as their industry contracts. Superficially, this seems highly plausible. But it does not necessarily follow in a long-run analysis of a low-income industry. Unskilled labour (and indeed management with skills not specific to furniture-making) may be better off if unemployment induces them to find more rewarding jobs elsewhere. The issue is more complex for other factors of production. Owners of a contracting industry become involved in once-and-for-all sunk-capital losses; on the other hand, the capital they do manage to extract may be invested in another industry yielding a higher return.[6] Labour and management with skills specific to the contracting industry may also become involved in sunk-capital losses,[7] along with higher income in new employment. The

---

[6]This may be important in furniture-making. There is evidence that a number of owners have kept their capital in this industry despite a depressed return.

[7]In this case, sunk capital is investment in training.

conclusion is that the long-run production effects of a contracting industry need not necessarily be unfavourable.

3. *Restricted single-industry free trade*

It has been concluded that complete across-the-board free trade is preferable to either of the partial schemes examined above. But if for political reasons this cannot be undertaken, some modified single-industry scheme may be considered. If there is an additional restraint that free trade can only be introduced if the existence of the industry is assured, then a limited scheme like the Automotive Agreement with its balance of payments or production constraints would become the active option. The essential difference between a limited auto-type scheme and an unrestricted single-industry plan is that the latter directs gains to the consumer, while the former initially directs gains to the producer.[8]

Provided domestic prices in Canada are reduced sufficiently to offset the duty loss to the taxpayer (as has been the case in the, admittedly tardy, auto precedent), a restricted single-industry scheme would leave the consumer no worse off than under present protection. Any net increase in production efficiency[9] would represent a windfall gain, which would initially go to the producer; this might eventually be distributed to the consumer (via further price cuts) or to labour (in higher wages) or as increased profits to owners. Hence, so long as it induces rationalization of the industry, such a scheme may be judged preferable to protection. However, problems would remain.

A. THE EQUITY ISSUE

Assurances of minimal necessary price reductions to the consumer[10] would have to be incorporated in such a scheme. Otherwise, the consumer/taxpayer might not be left equally well off, and this scheme would be complicated by equity issues arising from the redistribution of duty revenue from the taxpayer to the importer.

B. ADMINISTRATIVE PROBLEMS

Complications would arise if Canadian furniture producers were to become the sole agents for the import of U.S. furniture. For example, what would happen to present furniture importers? (Administrative problems have

---

[8]Eventually these gains may go to the labour force or the consumer.
[9]I.e., cost saving due to rationalization less changeover costs.
[10]I.e., sufficient to cover the reduction in government duty revenue. A simpler alternative would be the imposition by the government of a compensating sales tax; this could be covered by the producer from his duty savings without raising prices.

been minimized in the auto industry because that industry is characterized by parent-subsidiary ties.) Any marketing of a U.S. firm's output in Canada through a Canadian firm would raise anti-trust problems. Furthermore, marketing economies might induce the takeover of Canadian firms by U.S. companies. There would be other administrative problems as well; but these are not pursued, since they would be secondary to fundamental economic difficulties to which we now turn.

C. RATIONALIZATION OF CANADIAN INDUSTRY IN DOUBT

It is by no means certain that any windfall efficiency gains would come from such a scheme, since it is not clear that it would be profitable for the Canadian industry to increase volume by exploiting the duty-free U.S. market.

The option for a Canadian firm under such a scheme would be to specialize for export, while importing (duty-free) items of equal value in the lines it would be dropping from Canadian production. Its profit would come from the sale of U.S. imports in Canada and could run up to the 25 percent protection that would still remain as a price seal on the Canadian market.[11] However, there would be loss incurred on its export sales, since high-cost Canadian units would be sold in the United States at low prevailing prices there. This loss would initially be about 18 percent,[12] but with increased Canadian specialization might be reduced to about 8 or 9 percent.[13]

Thus manufacturers would incur losses on exports in order to make even greater profits on imports. From the social point of view, two windfalls would be involved for Canada, one of production and one of exchange. The production windfall is any increase in efficiency that results from more specialized production in Canada. The exchange windfall is the consumption gain involved in exchanging Canadian-built furniture[14] for U.S.-built furniture.[15] This suggests that, from either the social or the private point of view, this scheme is preferable to the present situation of protection.

There are a number of reasons why this favourable conclusion would

---

[11]And perhaps even higher; the inconvenience consumers would face in shopping in the United States might allow a price up to 40 percent above the U.S. level (see n. 5, chap. 5).

[12]I.e., Canadian furniture would be sold in the United States at a price about 18 percent below the price at which it is now sold in Canada (see Figure 1).

[13]I.e., the higher cost in Canada that would remain after rationalization. This is made up almost entirely of higher input costs that would remain in a single-industry scheme (D_m in Figure 1).

[14]Which the Canadian market now values, marginally, at 18 percent above the U.S. price.

[15]Which Canadians marginally value at 25–40 percent above the U.S. price (see n. 5, chap. 5).

need to be modified. If the consumer/taxpayer is to be reimbursed for his loss of duty revenue, furniture prices on *all* Canadian sales would have to be reduced by 1 or 2 percent.[16] A price reduction on a product involving so many complex, differentiated items would be extremely difficult to measure, let alone enforce. This price reduction would reduce the incentive facing a Canadian furniture-maker; his incentive would be further reduced by whatever costs he might face in marketing imports in Canada and in marketing his own lines in the United States.[17] It is therefore not clear that Canadian firms would rationalize to engage in export-import trade under an auto-type scheme.

D. THE CHOICE OF INDUSTRY

Regardless of whether or not rationalization occurs and windfall gains result, the authors do not recommend a restricted single-industry scheme for furniture. It is less desirable to introduce limited free trade in this industry than in almost any other—for a number of reasons.

(*a*) One rationale for such a scheme is that it provides protection and subsidy to ensure that an industry will survive during the period in which it is reorganizing; once efficiently set up, it can then weather real free trade. But if the government wishes to use subsidy measures to ensure the survival of an industry, it surely should select a high-income, rather than a low-income, industry. So long as the Americans are prepared to cooperate in such asymmetrical agreements, high-wage industries such as the auto industry should be chosen.[18]

(*b*) Not only is this a low-wage industry in Canada; it is also one of the few industries in which U.S. wages are about at the Canadian level, largely because Canadian furniture-makers in Ontario and Quebec are competing with a U.S. industry in North Carolina. Hence, in the event of eventual complete free trade, this industry is unlikely to be in as strong a competitive position as many other Canadian industries that do enjoy a wage advantage.

(*c*) This industry is very sensitive to higher-priced protected inputs. While this would not affect the industry in the event of across-the-board free trade, it does jeopardize any single-industry scheme. Accordingly, incen-

[16]The Canadian government would lose its present 25 percent duty on imports, which comprise about 6 percent of domestic consumption—a loss equivalent to 1.5 percent of total domestic sales (i.e., .25 × .06).

[17]The Canadian producer may find it difficult to market his product in the United States. Adequate sales staff, inventory maintenance, and advertising support would take time to develop. Furthermore, it might take time to adjust to the different technique of furniture wholesaling in the United States.

[18]The industry selected should be one capable of paying high wages (and other incomes) with unrestricted trade; logically, this need not be an industry which pays high wages under protection, although the two are likely to be the same.

tives might be insufficient to induce Canadian rationalization; and even if it were to occur, it would not spread back into major supplying industries (e.g., textiles). In the auto case, most important component suppliers could be incorporated into the scheme, and those that could not (e.g., steel) were selling at reasonably competitive prices in any case. In the furniture industry, some supply components could undoubtedly be included; but one of the most critical suppliers—textiles—is an industry in its own right and, indeed, an industry many times the size of furniture-making. It is difficult to see how it could be included without transforming the plan into a two-industry scheme.

4. *Comparison of options*

Of all the schemes discussed in this study, economic considerations indicate that unrestricted free trade in all industries should be preferred. Not only would efficiency gains be introduced in many industries rather than just in the furniture industry. In addition, reduced input prices would allow the furniture industry to compete more successfully.

A negotiated step-by-step move to free trade by all industries (e.g., a series of GATT bargaining rounds) would be less attractive, since the first such multilateral tariff reduction would be more effective in increasing import competition than in opening export markets.

If for political reasons it is feasible to introduce free trade in only one industry at a time, then the options become either an unrestricted single-industry plan (such as farm implements) or a restricted single-industry scheme (such as autos). However, if there is a further restriction that such a scheme must "prove successful" in terms of maintaining factor employment in that industry (rather than increasing real income of factors now in the industry), then there remains little choice. An auto-type scheme is indicated, since this is the only option that would ensure continued existence of a furniture industry.

But if economic choice is so restricted that only auto-type schemes may be undertaken, then furniture seems to be one of the last industries to qualify. Instead, the authorities should seek out industries in which (i) incomes are high in both countries, (ii) Canadian producers enjoy a substantial wage advantage, and (iii) Canadian input protection is relatively unimportant and/or inputs can easily be included in the scheme. Finally, industries selected should face a clear-cut inducement to rationalize, with strong competitive strength indicated if and when a final step to real free trade is undertaken. Substantial administrative difficulties might remain for industries selected on these grounds; but they are unlikely to be more severe than the administrative problems involved for the furniture industry.

7. The Path of Adjustment

1. *Problems and objectives*

Timing and adjustment assistance would be important determinants of the final success of any trade-liberalization program. In this section these issues are considered, and a proposal is set out for staging tariff reductions to unrestricted free trade.[1]

While the consumer wishes as rapid tariff reductions as possible, the issue is not as clear for the producer. Although some producers may favour rapid tariff reductions (e.g., to reduce input costs and open U.S. markets), some may not. Many may prefer delays to provide time for at least partial depreciation of any Canadian machinery and equipment that has been installed in the past to service Canadian markets but is inefficient under free trade. From the point of view of the firm, sunk-capital losses would be reduced, and firms would be in a stronger position to raise funds necessary for rationalization.

Hence there may be a conflict of interest between consumers and some producers. The speed of tariff removal may involve an implicit value judgment by the authorities on the strength of each case. But even if an extended staging process is chosen, it must not be so drawn out over time that it removes the incentive to reorganize. In this case, equipment inefficient by North American market standards might be reinstalled in Canada even after the staging process to free trade has begun.

Any proposed scheme should meet two primary objectives. First, it should encourage the most efficient to expand. Second, it should facilitate the re-employment of resources released by declining, inefficient firms. And the distinction between the efficient and the inefficient should be left to the market.

[1]It is assumed that tariffs on all manufactured goods are removed; however, the implications for the furniture industry only are considered.

2. *A possible scheme*

The present 25 percent Canadian tariff might be eliminated by a five-stage reduction of 5 percent per year.[2] This period would allow firms time to rationalize their output and marketing to the wider continental market. Furthermore, five years in the half-life of machinery in the industry;[3] while there is no timing sequence that would completely eliminate capital losses, this seems to be a reasonable guideline for limiting them.

Coincident with the first reduction in the tariff, an excise tax would be imposed on all furniture sold in Canada. This tax could be as much as the 5 percent reduction in the tariff and still leave the consumer as well off. On retail sales of $620 million,[4] the government would collect about $31 million in revenue. About $1 million would represent compensation for the loss in duty revenue because of the lower import tariff. The remainder could be used for relocation and retraining of any displaced labour and/or as an interim subsidy for firms in the industry. For example, tax exemption might be allowed on the base profits of firms in operation before the scheme was initiated. These base profits would be equal to their average annual profits earned in the five-year period prior to the initiation of this scheme; any additional profit would be taxed at the normal corporate rate. Such a policy would clearly encourage the efficient, but not the inefficient: no profit, no tax relief. This relief would be provided either to firms remaining in furniture-making or to those which exit. In the latter case, this tax credit would represent a major asset to bring to a new manufacturing activity. This tax relief could be further restricted to apply only if a certain percentage of value added is maintained in the present site of furniture-manufacturing. Such a policy is not strongly recommended in this study; however, if a high premium is placed on maintaining present small furniture towns, such a proviso could easily be incorporated.

This would not be a costly subsidy, since it would probably involve less than $5 million of tax remission.[5] A net addition of over $25 million in government revenue would remain. This could be used to subsidize increased output of furniture firms, a measure which would encourage expanding firms; these firms are more likely than not to be the relatively efficient.[6] Alternatively, this sum could be used to subsidize job retraining

[2]The U.S. tariff would also be eliminated at this rate, or faster if the Americans are willing.
[3]As allowed by the U.S. Internal Revenue Service.
[4]Estimated for 1965 from figures supplied by the Department of Industry.
[5]The 443 profit-earning firms filing a federal tax return in 1963 paid $2.8 million in corporate tax.
[6]But this is not guaranteed. Note that even corporate tax remission would not abso-

and relocation of the labour force; if used exclusively in this way, this subsidy would be equal to almost one-quarter of the recent industry payroll.[7] Which of these two additional subsidies is chosen would depend on a value judgment: the former is appropriate if a high premium is placed on maintaining the present Canadian industry structure and, in particular, a furniture industry; the second is appropriate if the objective is high-income employment of the labour force.

Such a scheme would initially direct all benefits to furniture firms and factors, rather than to the consumer. In subsequent years, as tariffs are further reduced, increased production subsidies would be possible, financed by an excise tax that could be as high as 10 percent in the second year, 15 percent in the third, and so on. Thus, the government's ability to subsidize would increase as the pressure of price competition from imports on the industry builds up. To what extent this should be entirely expended on subsidies to producers rather than to consumers would be an arbitrary judgment. But regardless of how justified production subsidies may be as an interim measure to ease reorganization of the industry, little case can be made for continuing them beyond the short term. Therefore, in the long run both the import tariff and the excise tax should be completely removed, with the consumer enjoying maximum benefits of free trade.

---

lutely guarantee a subsidy to the most efficient; for example, a very efficient firm may have had depressed profits in the base period prior to the scheme because of a costly reorganization for export. And there would be other problems; for example, in a diversified firm, how is total profit in the base period to be allocated between furniture-making and other activities?

[7]The industry payroll in 1962 was $121 million.

Appendices

Appendix A: Classification of furniture

Furniture is not a homogeneous good. The furniture industry is composed of separate subsectors with some common features, but more often differing greatly in inputs, outputs, and production techniques. There are three ways to subdivide the industry.

It can be divided by major input or component. Thus we would have the wooden-furniture portion ($126,232), metal furniture ($75,651), upholstered products ($71,323), and bedding ($38,051). The principal advantage of this classification is that it facilitates analysis of manufacturing techniques, costs, inputs, etc.

An alternative DBS classification scheme divides the industry by end use. This yields: household furniture ($219,996), office furniture ($37,764), and miscellaneous (including institutional furniture, bedding, and upholstered items) ($100,823). The advantage of this scheme is that it facilitates analysis of marketing problems and income, price, and demand relationships. But it makes analysis of component costs more difficult.

The third form of classification is the *de facto* ordering used in the industry. This classification is by component and end use as shown in Table AI. This scheme permits easy analysis of cost and input relationships as well as of marketing problems. Unfortunately, the data that are available are classified by the DBS end-use method. Problems of comparability of data frequently forced us to use higher levels of aggregation than was our original intent. It will be noted from the text that we generally used the industry's classification scheme, as shown in Table AI.

TABLE AI

Type of Furniture	Shipped in 1962
	($000)
Wooden houshold furniture (referred to as "case goods" by the industry); e.g., bedroom and dining-room furniture, end tables, and other occasional pieces	81,662
Wooden institutional furniture; e.g., school desks, church pews, etc.	32,786
Wooden office furniture; e.g., desks, filing cabinets, tables	11,784
Metal household furniture (referred to as "chrome ware" by the industry); e.g., dinette suites, metal frame chairs	30,138
Metal institutional furniture; e.g., hospital beds and tables, metal frame desks and chairs	21,813
Metal office furniture; e.g., desks, files, tables	21,070
Upholstered furniture; e.g., furniture more often than not used in the household. Some is used in institutions and business (such as hotels), but the bulk is in the form of sofas, chairs, and ottomans and is sold to households	71,323
Bedding; e.g., mattresses, pillows, and box springs	38,051
Total	308,627

Appendix B

TABLE B1

COMPARATIVE WAGES BY JOB CLASSIFICATION IN THE WOODEN-FURNITURE INDUSTRY
UNITED STATES AND CANADA, 1962
(in domestic dollars)

	U.S. region			Canadian region	
Job	Middle Atlantic	East North Central	South Atlantic	Quebec	Ontario
Assemblers, case goods	2.12	1.87	1.34	1.55	1.69
Cutoff saw operators	1.89	1.82	1.39	1.30	1.38
Gluers, rough stock	1.76	1.71	1.29	1.28	1.37
Maintenance men	1.50	1.54	1.21	1.03	1.25
Packers, furniture	1.73	1.64	1.27	1.13	1.30
Ripsaw operators	1.85	1.78	1.36	1.29	1.51
Rubbers, furniture	2.04	1.74	1.27	1.25	1.49
Sanders, furniture	1.79	1.73	1.37	1.27	1.40
Tenoner operators	1.98	1.99	1.53	1.42	1.58

Sources: U.S. data as of July, 1962: "Earnings in Wood Household Furniture, July 1962," *Monthly Labor Review,* July 1963, pp. 814–16.
Canadian Data: "Wooden Furniture," *Wage Rates, Salaries and Hours of Labour, 1962,* Report no. 45, Economic and Research Branch, Department of Labour, Ottawa, p. 113.

Comparisons and classifications may not be exact in all cases. The U.S. source lists twelve classifications, while the Canadian data have twenty-seven separate headings. But the evidence remains clear: Ontario wages are slightly higher, and Quebec wages slightly lower, than wages in the southeastern region of the United States.

RELATED PUBLICATIONS BY THE
PRIVATE PLANNING ASSOCIATION OF CANADA

CANADIAN TRADE COMMITTEE PUBLICATIONS

THE WORLD ECONOMY

The World Economy at the Crossroads: A Survey of Current Problems of Money, Trade and Economic Development, by Harry G. Johnson, 1965.
The International Monetary System: Conflict and Reform, by Robert A. Mundell, 1965.
International Commodity Agreements, by William E. Haviland, 1963.

CANADA'S TRADE RELATIONSHIPS

Canada's International Trade: An Analysis of Recent Trends and Patterns, by Bruce Wilkinson, 1968.
Canada's Trade with the Communist Countries of Eastern Europe, by Ian M. Drummond, 1966.
Canada's Role in Britain's Trade, by Edward M. Cape, 1965.
The Common Agricultural Policy of the E.E.C. and its Implications for Canada's Exports, by Sol Sinclair, 1964.
Canada's Interest in the Trade Problems of Less Developed Countries, by Grant L. Reuber, 1964.

CANADA'S COMMERCIAL POLICY AND COMPETITIVE POSITION

Prices, Productivity, and Canada's Competitive Position, by N. H. Lithwick, 1967.
Industrial Structure in Canada's International Competitive Position: A Study of the Factors Affecting Economies of Scale and Specialization in Canadian Manufacturing, by H. Edward English, 1964.
Canada's Approach to Trade Negotiations, by L. D. Wilgress, 1963.

CANADIAN-AMERICAN COMMITTEE PUBLICATIONS

CANADA-U.S. ECONOMIC RELATIONS

Constructive Alternatives to Proposals for U.S. Import Quotas (a Statement by the Committee), 1968.
U.S.-Canadian Free Trade: The Potential Impact on the Canadian Economy, by Paul Wonnacott and Ronald J. Wonnacott, 1968.
The Role of International Unionism in Canada, by John H. G. Crispo, 1967.
A New Trade Strategy for Canada and the United States (a Statement by the Committee), 1966.
Capital Flows between Canada and the United States, by Irving Brecher, 1965.
A Possible Plan for a Canada-U.S. Free Trade Area (a Staff Report), 1965.
Invisible Trade Barriers between Canada and the United States, by Francis Masson and H. Edward English, 1963.
Non-Merchandise Transactions between Canada and the United States, by John W. Popkin, 1963.
Policies and Practices of United States Subsidiaries in Canada, by John Lindeman and Donald Armstrong, 1961.

Lightning Source UK Ltd.
Milton Keynes UK
UKHW012358200722
406167UK00001B/306